"I am grateful that Chuck DeGroat wrote this book. He [...] write it and *the* person I would want as a guide on this issue. Chuck has a wealth of wisdom to offer as he has counseled those with narcissistic personality disorder as well as the those deeply wounded by narcissistic leaders. This book is filled with compassion for both narcissists and those affected by the destructive power of narcissism."

Justin S. Holcomb, Episcopal priest, seminary professor, and coauthor of *Rid of My Disgrace: Hope and Healing for Victims of Sexual Assault*

"If you wonder why family and friends have left the church or why you often feel more lost than found when you step into the sanctuary, this book is for you. Whether you're the pastor or the parishioner, Chuck DeGroat, asks the stark-raving honest questions about church and church leadership that most of us are afraid to voice, even though they simmer in our hearts and leave us hot with confusion and emptiness. This book will not challenge you to pick up stones and throw them through stained-glass windows, but it will engage you to look within and find your true North Star to follow through the wilderness of church to an authentic spirituality of living, serving, worshipping, inviting, and communing in love tethered to something far greater than our small denominations, building programs, or evangelism crusades—to Someone far greater than ourselves."

Sharon A. Hersh, therapist and author of *The Last Addiction: Why Self-Help is Not*

"Why are we just beginning to talk about narcissism in our spiritual leaders? Chuck DeGroat believes it is because we have been rewarding it in our churches. He is powerfully and painfully right! More than just calling out narcissism, DeGroat skillfully unpacks how it shows up in leaders of large and small churches, beloved Christian celebrities, and seemingly godly men and women. *When Narcissism Comes to Church* peels back the layers, ever so carefully on our 'real selves.' We need this pastoral-surgical work. Trust the sage guidance offered by Chuck DeGroat, taking us through our illusions into the healing our souls and systems desperately need."

Dan White Jr., author of *Love Over Fear*, cofounder of the Praxis Gathering

"I don't even want to venture a guess as to why I was asked to endorse this book. Chuck DeGroat's latest feels like 'a double-edged sword. It penetrates even to dividing soul and spirit, joints and marrow; it judges the thoughts and attitudes of the heart.' Chuck handles his pastoral scalpel with surgical precision, cutting, stripping, and trimming where I need it the most."

Tim Blackmon, chaplain, Wheaton College

"If you, like so many, have been lured in by the shiny veneer of narcissism only to be left shattered, confused, and filled with shame, you will find help in these pages. In *When Narcissism Comes to Church*, Chuck DeGroat nimbly pulls back the veil—exposing the many faces of narcissism and helping us see what lies underneath. Drawing on decades of experience, DeGroat writes with honesty, wisdom, and compassion, providing help for the wounded and hope for the church."

Alison Cook, therapist and coauthor of *Boundaries for Your Soul*

"A book on this topic is desperately needed right now. But more than that, we need a deeply thoughtful treatise on this subject that also points a healthy way forward. This is that book. Every one of us can learn something from Chuck's words, but more importantly we can gain the courage needed to face this destructive force in our churches."

Nancy Ortberg, CEO of Transforming the Bay with Christ

WHEN NARCISSISM
COMES TO CHURCH

HEALING YOUR COMMUNITY FROM
EMOTIONAL AND SPIRITUAL ABUSE

CHUCK DeGROAT

FOREWORD BY RICHARD J. MOUW

An imprint of InterVarsity Press
Downers Grove, Illinois

InterVarsity Press
P.O. Box 1400 | Downers Grove, IL 60515-1426
ivpress.com | email@ivpress.com

InterVarsity Press® is the publishing division of InterVarsity Christian Fellowship/USA®. For more information, visit intervarsity.org.

Scripture quotations, unless otherwise noted, are from the New Revised Standard Version Bible, copyright © 1989 National Council of the Churches of Christ in the United States of America. Used by permission. All rights reserved worldwide.

While any stories in this book are true, some names and identifying information may have been changed to protect the privacy of individuals.

The publisher cannot verify the accuracy or functionality of website URLs used in this book beyond the date of publication.

Cover design and image composite: David Fassett
Interior design: Daniel van Loon

ISBN 978-1-5140-0509-5 (paperback) | ISBN 978-0-8308-4159-2 (hardcover) |
ISBN 978-0-8308-4199-8 (digital)

Printed in the United States of America ∞

Library of Congress Cataloging-in-Publication Data
Names: DeGroat, Chuck, author.
Title: When narcissism comes to church : healing your community from emotional and spiritual abuse/ Chuck DeGroat; foreword by Richard J. Mouw.
Description: Downers Grove, Illinois : IVP, an imprint of InterVarsity Press, 2020. | Includes bibliographical references.
Identifiers: LCCN 2019052381 (print) I LCCN 2019052382 (ebook) I ISBN 9780830841592 (hardcover) I ISBN 9780830841998 (ebook)
Subjects: LCSH: Clergy–Psychology. I Narcissism–Religious aspects–Christianity. I Psychological abuse–Religious aspects–Christianity. I Pastoral theology.
Classification: LCC BV4398 .D44 2020 (print) I LCC BV4398 (ebook) I DDC 253/.2–dc23
LC record available at https://lccn.loc.gov/2019052381
LC ebook record available at https://lccn.loc.gov/2019052382

29 28 27 26 25 24 23 | 13 12 11 10 9 8 7 6 5 4 3 2

The pleasure that is in his heart when he does difficult things and succeeds in doing them well, tells him secretly: "I am a saint." At the same time, others seem to recognize him as different from themselves. They admire him, or perhaps avoid him—a sweet homage of sinners! The pleasure burns into a devouring fire. The warmth of that fire feels very much like the love of God. It is fed by the same virtues that nourished the flame of charity. He burns with self-admiration and thinks: "It is the fire of the love of God." He thinks his own pride is the Holy Ghost. The sweet warmth of pleasure becomes the criterion of all his works. The relish he savors in acts that make him admirable in his own eyes, drives him to fast, or to pray, or to hide in solitude, or to write many books, or to build churches and hospitals, or to start a thousand organizations. And when he gets what he wants he thinks his sense of satisfaction is the unction of the Holy Spirit. And the secret voice of pleasure sings in his heart: "Now sum sicut caeteri homines" (I am not like other men). Once he has started on this path there is no limit to the evil his self-satisfaction may drive him to do in the name of God and of His love, and for His glory. He is so pleased with himself that he can no longer tolerate the advice of another—or the commands of a superior. When someone opposes his desires he folds his hands humbly and seems to accept it for the time being, but in his heart he is saying: "I am persecuted by worldly men. They are incapable of understanding one who is led by the Spirit of God. With the saints it has always been so." Having become a martyr he is ten times as stubborn as before. It is a terrible thing when such a one gets the idea he is a prophet or a messenger of God or a man with a mission to reform the world. . . . He is capable of destroying religion and making the name of God odious to men.

Thomas Merton, *New Seeds of Contemplation*

CONTENTS

Richard J. Mouw

C huck DeGroat and I have been together on several occasions, and we have also corresponded about matters of mutual interest, but I can't say that we know each other well. While reading this marvelously insightful book, however, I had the sense that I was having a conversation with a close friend about worship services and meetings—and more than one private encounter with married couples!—where he and I had both been present. That he assigns fictional names to the persons in the case studies he narrates even tempted me at several points to give real names to the folks in his stories.

My frequent aha experiences in reading what he has written signals that he is discussing issues that are all too familiar to those of us who pay even minimal attention to what is going on these days in the Christian community and the larger culture. As I was reading this book, I was struck by how often news reports and casual conversations include the word *narcissistic*. This is a book that speaks to matters that are the stuff of our daily lives.

To be sure, Chuck does more here than simply remind us of things that are familiar. For me, his insights come from a perspective that is well beyond my own area of expertise. I am in awe of how he combines pastoral experience with a grasp of psychological theory and therapeutic savvy. And he does this—and here I *can* claim some expertise—with solid theology.

There is much in these pages that inform us about different aspects and types of narcissistic personalities. What I find most helpful, though, is the way he probes beneath the surface of these categorizations. Early on, for example, he cites Christopher Lasch's provocative observation that narcissism is the "longing to be free from longing," a path that some individuals pursue to distance themselves from their humanity. This points us to the profound Augustinian insistence that we humans are created with restless spirits that can only find fulfillment in a healthy relationship with the living God. Narcissism, as is clear throughout these pages, is one means that individuals employ to alienate themselves from their true humanness.

There is some tough material in this book. Chuck rightly complains that narcissism among pastoral leaders is an understudied reality, and he charts out corrective measures by alerting us to warning signs. With the toughness, though, also comes hope, as he provides concrete evidence that narcissists themselves can find paths toward wholeness. But the hope offered here is not only for the hardcore narcissist. Chuck rightly urges all of us to engage in the difficult "shadow work" that requires directly confronting the darker sides of our individual psyches. When we do, he promises, we can discover in the darkness some of the "holy longings" that God has implanted in us for the journey toward finding our true humanity.

INTRODUCTION

Narcissist. It's a word we toss around today, perhaps too lightly, about politicians and pastors, celebrities and sports personalities. I do it. You do it. Perhaps there is some power in being able to diagnose, to label what both mystifies and terrifies.

This became a kind of sport during the 2016 election cycle, when Donald J. Trump found himself in the crosshairs of both amateur and professional diagnosticians. Among many others, John Gartner, a Johns Hopkins University Medical School psychologist, made the controversial contention that the leader of the free world is a "malignant narcissist," demonstrating features of aggressiveness, paranoia, grandiosity, manipulation, entitlement, projection, and more.[1] It's not my task to diagnose the leader of the free world. But it's true enough—narcissism in the public sphere can be dramatic and grand, a spectacle to behold, and even traumatic to experience.

When we experience narcissism personally and relationally, the toxic effects are painful and crazy-making. Perhaps he's the church planter whose charm and sense of authority appears compelling but whose leadership style produces a relational debris field. Or the spouse whose controlling behavior makes you feel unsafe and crazy. Or the committee chairwoman whose team walks on eggshells. When narcissism invades the space of family, work, or church life, the impact is dramatic and traumatic. That's why I think a book like this is important. We need to talk.

But it's not enough to look at narcissism through the lens of an egotistical political figure or an emotionally abusive spouse, an arrogant CEO, or a powerful religious figure. We swim in the cultural waters of narcissism, and churches are not immune. Western culture is a *narcissistic culture*, as Christopher Lasch declared decades ago in his famous book *The Culture of Narcissism*. The same vacuousness we see beneath an individual's narcissistic grandiosity can be found at a collective level in American culture, evidenced most recently in the #MeToo and #ChurchToo movements. While we tell ourselves stories of American exceptionalism, we hide what's beneath—fragmentation, systemic racism, ethnocentrism, misogyny, addiction, shame, and so much more. We've got a problem—all of us. It's an *us* problem, not a *them* problem. My hope is that this book will invite each of us to ask how we participate in narcissistic systems while providing clear resources for those traumatized by narcissistic relationships, particularly in the church.

Late in *The Culture of Narcissism*, Lasch defines narcissism as the "longing to be freed from longing."[2] In other words, the narcissist cannot tolerate the limitations of his humanity. What Lasch seems to be saying is that narcissism is about control. It is a refusal to live within God-ordained limitations of creaturely existence. Paradoxically, our desire to be superhuman dehumanizes us, wreaking havoc on our relationships.

Yes, narcissism makes us *less* human. Eventually the masks meant to protect ourselves and ease the ache of our longings become the only faces we know. The face of narcissism seems to work in Western culture, and sadly it's a face that many churchgoers look to for spiritual inspiration and motivation.

I began studying narcissism in the late 1990s. We were not talking about narcissistic leadership in the church then, and sadly we're still only on the cusp of that conversation now. I began studying it because I was seeing it in myself, in my classmates from seminary, and in my colleagues in ministry. Church planting was ramping up in my denomination at that time, and in the spirit of mission it seemed as if we were sweeping psychological health under the rug. I've experienced my own share of trauma under narcissistic leadership.[3] It seemed then as if few had a category for narcissism's uniquely diabolical complexion, and twenty years later the church is still tragically underinformed.

So I launched into my own study, accompanied by lots of therapy to make sense of the wounds I had experienced. I studied narcissism in dozens of cases and in key books and recognized it as a growing phenomenon. In his book *The Depleted Self: Sin in a Narcissistic Age,* Donald Capps described the shift from a guilt-anxiety society to a shame-narcissism society.[4] The connection to shame was immediately intriguing to me, as it seemed to be connected to many of the issues I was seeing in Christian men in particular—pornography or alcohol addictions, workaholism, vocational unrest, spiritual doubt, and depression.[5]

In the popular book *Healing the Shame That Binds You,* John Bradshaw reinforced Capps's thesis and packaged it in a way that launched it onto the *New York Times* bestseller list and brought the shame conversation out of the psychoanalytic shadows. Bradshaw traced the origins of shame in a way that helped me see it as jet fuel for narcissists. Buttressed by the work of Alexander Lowen in *Narcissism: Denial of the True Self,* I began to see how disconnected those with narcissistic personality disorder (NPD) are from their core feelings and true selves, living from a compensatory part of themselves that shields them from the shame and pain within.[6] Understanding narcissism's underbelly has been the most important revelation for my own work with pastors, ministry leaders, spouses, and organizations. As you'll see, this revelation invites us to take narcissism with a deadly seriousness, but also to envision a compassionate path forward.

As I learned—not just from the research but from the living experiences of women and men impacted by narcissism—I became convinced that narcissism was not only a growing reality but a misdiagnosed one, especially in churches. Indeed, within churches a narcissist might even be described as charismatic, gifted, confident, smart, strategic, agile, and compelling. He was selected to plant the church, to lead the ministry, to teach the class. He was quickly let off the hook when a spouse reported emotional abuse.

I saw also that it wasn't easy to confront systemic narcissism in churches that are seen as successful, special, blessed, Spirit led, and anointed. Whole church systems and programs evolve within the waters of narcissism, and when it's the water you swim in, it's hard to see and even harder to confront.

I'm convinced that my particular context—the United States— is a fertile soil for narcissism. Over thirty years ago, Eugene Peterson penned these words in his little-known book *Earth and Altar: The Community of Prayer in a Self-Bound Society:*

> On the "ribbon of highway" that stretches "from California to the New York Island"—the great American Main Street— the mass of people seem completely self-absorbed. One hundred and fifty years ago Alexis de Tocqueville visited America from France and wrote: "Each citizen is habitually engaged in contemplation of a very puny object, namely himself." In a century and a half things have not improved.

For all the diverse and attractive, buzzing and mysterious reality that is everywhere evident, no one and no thing interrupt people more than momentarily from obsessive preoccupation with themselves.[7]

Ministry leaders and churches today are obsessively preoccupied with their reputation, influence, success, rightness, progressiveness, relevance, platform, affirmation, and power. And research shows that narcissism is a growing phenomenon, particularly over the last fifty years. Baby Boomers had markedly higher narcissism scores than college students of the 1950s—and each subsequent generation has seen a rise. A comprehensive study from 2009 showed that incidences of narcissism had more than doubled in the prior ten years, with a growing number of women experiencing it as well.[8] Another substantial 2008 study showed a NPD prevalence of 7.7 percent in men and 4.8 percent in women.[9] As we'll soon see, instances of narcissism among pastors are much more common.

Today, the millennials have become targets of the label. They're seen as entitled and deemed the "Me Generation," with alarming statistics to make the case.[10] Some argue that millennials want special privileges, feel entitled to break the rules, and often demand more than others older than them.[11] Because many of my students are millennials, I get a bit defensive for them. Positively, I see them as less prone to take abuse, ignore an injustice, or minimize a feeling. Even still, I see that their avatar presence across many social media platforms and frenzied engagement in too many tasks mask deep questions of self-worth and belonging.[12] Their emergence as pastors and ministry leaders will invite more questions, revealing the ever-changing face of narcissism.

As a Gen-Xer, I can still remember the *Saturday Night Live* episode in 1991 when the now former senator Al Franken made his first appearance as Stuart Smalley, with his mock self-help show called *Daily Affirmations*. Smalley would look into his mirror and recite his mantra—"I'm good enough, I'm smart enough, and doggone it, people like me."[13] I grew up with President Reagan taking us out of the post-Vietnam and Watergate doldrums with his movie-star charm and "you-can-do-it" attitude, accompanied by a growing market of health, wealth, and success coming from television personalities, enlightened psychological gurus, and spiritual leaders, including self-described Christian ministers.

I am convinced that the missional fervor and rise in church planting we've witnessed since the 1980s can be correlated with the growing prevalence of narcissism. Nowhere have I seen the narcissism-shame dynamic more pronounced than among church planters, some of whom have become megachurch pastors. Some church planting assessments I've seen practically invite narcissistic leadership. My work in this area as a therapist, pastor, consultant, psychological assessor, and professor over many years persuades me that the narcissism in many young men in particular is baptized as spiritual giftedness in a way that does a great disservice to them and ignores deep wells of shame and fragility lurking within. If Lasch is right and narcissism is the "longing to be freed from longing," then each subsequent generation has found yet a new way to distance itself from its humanity, from its limitations. Each generation finds new ways to mask its fragility behind a shiny veneer. We avoid and evade our "real selves," as the noted personality-disorder theorist James Masterson put it.[14] Our great sin is that we run from the beauty of our God-given, God-gifted, God-loved reality as image bearers—humans designed to be enough without all of this extra baggage. Thomas Merton says it well:

All sin starts from the assumption that my false self, the self that exists only in my own egocentric desires, is the fundamental reality of life around which everything else in the universe is ordered. Thus I use up my life in the desire for pleasures and the thirst for experiences, for power, honor, knowledge, feeling loved, in order to clothe this false self and construct its nothingness into something objectively real. And I wind experiences around myself and cover myself with pleasures and glory like bandages in order to make myself perceptible to myself and to the world.[15]

We play the Genesis 3 record on repeat. Though our narcissism has evolved, we're still living the same old story, told to us from time immemorial, of human beings who did not feel like they were enough, who wondered whether God might be holding out on them, who chose to listen to the serpent's whisper rather than God's declaration of goodness. Our flight from our humanity, as it turns out, is not very new at all. Our narcissism appears in different forms as we live out all of the other selves, which we are constantly "putting on and taking off like coats and hats against the world's weather."[16]

And yet deep within there is also the whisper of shalom for our own lives and for our relationships. Because the divine design is beautifully relational, imaging the beloved life of the Trinity, we can't seem to quit on hope. Somehow those who name themselves as followers of Jesus are haunted by a vision of restoration and wholeness. Sure, there are days when we'd rather resign ourselves to a more tragic story ("you're not worth it"), but the problem is this: God doesn't quit on us. He continues pursuing, in Jesus, by the Spirit, longing for us to know that we are loved, valued, brimming with dignity.

And this has implications for the language I use in this book. Because each person is created in God's image, we cannot reduce people to a label or claim to fully understand them based on one predominant part of their personality. Human beings are "fearfully and wonderfully made" (Psalm 139:14). The biblical story defines human beings by their divinely dignified identity first and foremost, and thus sin is secondary, contingent, a disease of the soul. We must resist relegating anyone to a label, whether "narcissist" or "alcoholic," "anxious" or "depressed." In her masterful work on personality disorders, Elinor Greenberg writes, "Nobody is a Borderline. Nobody is a Narcissist. Nobody is a Schizoid. This may seem a strange way to begin a book on diagnosis, but it needs to be said. When we diagnose, we are describing a pattern, a particular Gestalt, never a person. All people are unique. Labels, however well intended, cannot do justice to human complexity."[17]

Yet narcissism is real. And for this reason, I do not resist naming a person as a "narcissist"—not as the definitive label describing their true, ontological self, but as a description of a pattern of living and relating. The heart is prone to deceit (Jeremiah 17:9), and contemporary psychology has done us the service of naming our heart's deceits as pathological patterns of relating, often born out of life's brokenness and shame. As a mental health professional, I seek to use the term wisely and carefully. While mental health resources on the internet are helpful, they've also empowered us with a wide vocabulary and the power to place labels on friends, politicians, and people we're curious about, with or without professional discernment.

So I encourage wisdom and patience with labels. Ultimately, a descriptor like "narcissist" names the *persona*, the mask, a part of someone, but like other descriptors (doctor, father, diabetic, autistic) it does not account for our core "true self" hidden with

Christ in God. I hope my use of the words *narcissist* or *narcissism* shows both honesty and compassion.

This book has been twenty-plus years in the making, but my passion to write it comes from the courageous women and men I've worked with, whose stories of shame, brokenness, hope, and healing live in me and inform every aspect of my work. I dedicate this book to them. My belief is that God desires truth in our inner being (Psalm 51:6) and that this truth has the power to transform our lives, our churches, our relationships, and our society. Dismantling the narcissistic false self is an act of dying—dying to illusion, to control, and to fear. And it's also an act of resurrection—to truth, to vulnerability, to creativity, and to connection. As we trust that Love desires the best for us, and not our downfall, perhaps we'll all tire of the masks we wear and come out of hiding. May all of us committed to this work know the freedom that comes as we step out from shadows into the light.

CHAPTER ONE

WHEN NARCISSISM COMES TO CHURCH

Appear to be what thou art, tear off thy masks.
The church was never meant to be a masquerade.

Charles Spurgeon

I n my high school youth group, we were asked to memorize Philippians 2. The heading in my Bible back then said something like "Imitating Christ's Humility." The invitation to humility was predicated on that of Christ,

> who, though he was in the form of God,
> did not regard equality with God
> as something to be exploited,
> but emptied himself,
> taking the form of a slave,
> being born in human likeness.
> And being found in human form,
> he humbled himself
> and became obedient to the point of death—
> even death on a cross. (Philippians 2:6-8)

Naively, I assumed most Christians were all about navigating this humble way. So when I met my first Christian "celebrity" while still in high school, I expected an incarnation of Jesus. On stage, he wooed and wowed, with arms waving and a smile so big you could see it from the back row of the auditorium. When I met him in person afterward, however, he was distant and cold—far from a Jesus incarnation—and way above a conversation with some teenage fan, too self-important for trivial encounters like this one.

On that day, I first encountered narcissism's ugly bite. I felt small and worthless—too insignificant even for a brief conversation. I wondered what was wrong, what he didn't see in me. Narcissism's bite always seems to leave you asking, "What's wrong with me?"

Narcissism came to church for me that day. I didn't have a descriptor for it, but I had the ugly aftertaste of a narcissistic encounter. About ten years later, narcissism's bite returned with a vengeance, this time from a charming and charismatic ministry peer whose affirmations of me would cause my soul to soar, but whose secretive, suspicious, and sometimes sinister machinations confused and even frightened me. After a season of feeling crazy, I sat with a therapist who said in no uncertain terms: "You're dealing with a narcissist."

A what? I didn't have the psychological vocabulary back then. The word was vaguely familiar, likely from the ecclesial and political scandals rocking the nation in the '90s. My therapist started connecting the dots. I felt crazy. I felt scared. I blamed myself. I felt like I had irreconcilable truths about this person's goodness and evil.

The picture that unfolded before me was far more complicated and crazy-making: a smart, seemingly wise and influential person in my life who was at the same time manipulative, abusive, and conniving. Charm and rage. Wisdom and folly. Righteousness and wickedness. Jekyll and Hyde.

In the coming months, my trust in humanity wavered. I began to see the dynamics of narcissism playing out in spiritually and emotionally abusive relationships from my earliest memories, through my formative college years, and into my seminary experience. For a season I became overly suspicious and judgmental of everyone. "Narcissist" became a label I'd brand people with far too freely. In my counselor training program, we'd toss around diagnostic categories liberally: "I'm seeing my borderline client tonight" or "I've got my sex addict at 4 p.m." In time I realized that this was a form of power: a way of coping with my feelings of insecurity and disappointment. Health and healing in my own journey, I realized, could not come from simply flipping the script and becoming the powerful one, armed with clinical categories and a new expertise to judge others. I'd need to confront my own latent narcissism.

Of course, we're all susceptible to narcissistic behavior. There are times when we all feel superior. We lay in bed at night thinking we deserve more. We compare and compete. These are general traits that might be shared by someone who is narcissistic. But narcissistic personality disorder (NPD) is something far more serious, characterized by grandiosity, entitlement, a need for admiration, and a lack of empathy. Those who are diagnosably narcissistic may be talented, charming, even inspiring, but they lack the capacity for self-awareness and self-evaluation, shunning humility for defensive self-protection. Christian psychologist Diane Langberg says of the narcissist, "He has many gifts but the gift of humility."[1]

While it seems as if the church should be the last place narcissism shows up, it does indeed—in ordinary laypeople, in clergy across all theological spectrums, and in systems that protect narcissistic people and foster abuse. Let's begin our exploration together by looking at each of these in turn.

THE NARCISSIST IN YOUR CHURCH

When we come to church, we often hide behind spiritual masks with smiles that cover our pain. As a client of mine once said, "I'm more myself on Wednesday nights at the church than on Sunday mornings." He was referring to his Wednesday Alcoholics Anonymous meetings.

The nineteenth-century preacher Charles Spurgeon once said, "Appear to be what thou art, tear off thy masks. The church was never meant to be a masquerade. Stand out in thy true colors."[2] I suspect the "Prince of Preachers" didn't own a *Diagnostic and Statistical Manual of Mental Disorders*, but he hints at an important dynamic—hiddenness is the breeding ground for narcissism. You ask why churches are breeding grounds for abuse and coverups, and I'll offer an epidemic of hiding. It's as old as Genesis 3, so we shouldn't be surprised.

I've seen this in spades over the years. Consider a couple that looked and dressed the part in their affluent suburban church, but whose narcissistic and abusive relationship was masked for years.[3] Years ago, I worked with Jade, a lifelong Christian and wife of twenty-three years to Vance. Many would say they were the model Christian couple, serving in various ways both up front and behind the scenes, and proud of their three beautiful teenaged kids. He was a successful doctor. She was a stay-at-home mom. She came to me for counseling to address what she considered to be depression around her daughter's impending move away to college, but it didn't take long for the tears to come in a torrent. There was much more going on.

Jade began to describe a long-time pattern of emotional abuse, though she didn't have those technical words. She walked on eggshells with a husband who was controlling and condescending. For years he'd criticized her weight, her cooking, her friendships, her faith. Over time she awakened to this toxic dynamic, eventually naming it to her husband as a significant problem in their marriage. She appealed to church leaders for help as Vance evaded hard conversations, and she began to share her story with a few safe friends.

Jade and Vance were essentially hidden for a decade in their church. They spent years in a small group. Friends had seen Vance publicly scold Jade, even taking her aside during a small group meeting to lay into her for not cooking enough food. On a dime, however, he'd revert back to the larger-than-life, charismatic charlatan that he was. She'd shrink, smiling along, ever the submissive wife. The church showed little support, even as she made repeated requests to different pastors asking for their intervention. There were whispers of her "mental instability" among some. She eventually resigned herself to an abusive marriage and discontinued counseling. Years later I saw her in the supermarket. She smiled as she passed by, hiding her pain even from one of the few people who knew its depths.

Or consider Beth. Beth served as an elder at a large church. She worked her way into the inner circle of leaders with her ingratiating and charming ways. Once in, she made herself so indispensable that some argued that she was an unpaid staff member, while others thought the church might fall apart without her genius and savvy. Over time, she fostered a narrative that the senior pastor was inept and incapable of growing the church, leading to the pastor's resignation.

Gradually, Beth's grand plan began to come into view. She proposed calling her good friend and former pastor in another state, a married man with whom she'd been intimately involved in the past. His own narcissistic tendencies had come onto the radar of his local presbytery, and he was ready to move. Evading accountability, he was called to Beth's church, with Beth pulling the strings all the while.

These two stories serve to illustrate how narcissism plays itself out among ordinary people in ordinary congregations. Most people in both churches were blind to the realities of the situations, but there were clear victims, obvious manipulation, and profound pain. The previous pastor at Beth's church didn't reenter ministry. Jade never did get the help she needed. Vance and Beth were both formidable people, whose big personalities and crafty ways won people over—even those who wondered at times if they could be trusted. Sadly, many of us naively trust the Vances and Beths of the world. They are convincing. They are charming. They are certain. And tragically they are deemed credible.

NARCISSISTIC PASTORS

The beloved priest-psychologist Henri Nouwen wasn't trying to define narcissism, but he might as well have been, when he wrote:

> The long painful history of the Church is the history of people ever and again tempted to choose power over love, control over the cross, being a leader over being led. Those who resisted this temptation to the end and thereby give us hope are the true saints. One thing is clear to me: the temptation of power is greatest when intimacy is a threat. Much Christian leadership is exercised by people who do not know how to develop healthy, intimate relationships and have opted for power and control instead. Many Christian empire-builders have been people unable to give and receive love.[4]

This sad abandonment of the humble way of Jesus shows up today in pastors of large and small churches, in beloved Christian celebrities, prolific clergy authors and bloggers, dynamic church planters, and seemingly godly men and women. The frightening reality of narcissism is that it often presents in a compelling package. Narcissism is the "glittering image" we present to the world, as novelist Susan Howatch describes it in her novel *Glittering Images*, which tells the story of a mid-twentieth century clergy narcissist.[5] Could it be that the very men and women who are called to be shepherds of the flock struggle most with narcissism?

Sadly, narcissism in the clergy is under studied. When I did my doctoral work over a decade ago, I discovered vast resources on pastoral well-being, including studies on burnout, addiction, and depression. I found popular articles on narcissistic leadership but an absence of studies on the prevalence of narcissism. I had a sense that we didn't want the world to know our dirty little secret. When I started doing psychological assessments for pastors and church planters, I saw that narcissistic traits were often presented as strengths. Narcissism can be interpreted as confidence, strong leadership, clear vision, a thick skin.

A colleague of mine often says that ministry is a magnet for a narcissistic personality—who else would want to speak on behalf of God every week? While the vast majority of people struggle with public speaking, not only do pastors do it regularly, but they do it with "divine authority." In my own work, which includes fifteen years of psychological testing among pastors, the vast majority of ministerial candidates test on the spectrum of Cluster B *DSM-V* personality disorders, which feature narcissistic traits most prominently (as we'll see in the next chapter). The rates are even higher among church planters.

Elevations on the narcissistic spectrum are coupled with testimonies that include fear of major failure (often moral failure), profound shame, and secret addictions. Hidden in the heart of these shepherds is profound shame. Power keeps the shame and fear at bay—at least for some time. The narcissistic mask is an armor of self-protection that both defends the fragile self within, but offends, oppresses, and alienates the other.

Narcissist pastors are anxious and insecure shepherds who do not lead the sheep to still waters but into hurricane winds. I've attended and spoken at dozens of pastor's conferences, and I see this anxiety abuzz in the comparison and competition, the showmanship and dress, the addictions to substances and fitness and social media and approval. I hear it in the anxious voice of a young pastor who was recently contacted by a literary agent and proudly proclaimed, "It's my time. Now I launch!" I feel it in the inauthenticity of a prospective church planter whose overly optimistic answers to my sincere queries about his health leave me wondering whether he's ever been honest with anyone. I sense it in the endless selfie posts of a trendy clergywoman whose daily social media displays seem to be a cry of "notice me." I see it in the veteran pastor who deems himself wise and enlightened and speaks with condescension to young staff members.

In my lifetime, the classic image of the devoted parish pastor who could be trusted to rightly preach the word, diligently care for souls, and wisely lead the church has shifted dramatically. With major scandals in both Protestant and Catholic churches, trust in clergy is down significantly over the last twenty years. Clergy trust has "dropped steadily since 2009, down from a high of 67 percent in 1985, the pollster reported. Pastors are now seen as less trustworthy than judges (43%), day care providers (46%), police officers (56%), pharmacists (62%), medical doctors (65%), grade school teachers (66%), military officers (71%), and nurses (82%)."[6]

Seminaries tasked with training the next generation of ordained clergy are also in decline.[7] Amidst scandals ranging from televangelists to Catholic priests to megachurch superstars, the pastorate is no longer seen as a noble vocation as it once was. Given this general decline, there is even greater pressure for those pursuing ministry to be good enough, smart enough, winsome enough, inspiring enough, and confident enough to bring revitalization, start new churches, and draw the dechurched back. The vocation of parish pastor is not as sexy as it once was.[8]

Interestingly, in my earliest years in ministry serving as a hybrid pastor-therapist, I was often asked to write references for prospective planters. My warnings about their narcissism were often read as recommendations of their gifts to inspire, their quick wit, strong leadership, charisma, charm, and influence. In retrospect, I see the damage done by those deemed ready to lead and plant churches. In too many postdenominational ministry networks today, where traditional ordination processes have been abandoned, young leaders are snatched up and deployed without proper training or soul formation, simply because they've been successful in other arenas.

We've not yet learned. But as stories of damaging narcissism increase, and as social media serves as an amplifier for victim's voices, we may be approaching a reckoning.

NARCISSISTIC CHURCHES

For centuries, ecclesial systems have been structured hierarchically, privileging particular people over others. Male leaders, the educated, people with resources, or the well-connected traditionally have greater access to power than others. Structures are not necessarily to blame for narcissism, but particular structures do create an environment where it can grow unchallenged.

Historically, Christendom's conflation of church and empire undermined the "kenotic configuration" of the church, replacing cruciform humility with hierarchy, patriarchy, and power.[9] The grandiosity, entitlement, and absence of empathy characteristic of narcissistic personality disorder was translated into the profile of a good leader.[10] Those affected by narcissism's bite were led to believe it was their fault—a lack of humility, a failure to submit. Systems of power and wealth that fostered abuse were perpetuated from generation to generation, even as leaders came and went.

Narcissistic systems thrive in structures that prop up those with authority and persona, while subordinating others according to gender, social status, theological understanding, perceived giftedness (or lack thereof), ability, and more.[11] What's more, these systems perpetuate shame among those who are not as holy, connected, charismatic, intelligent, or powerful. This insider-outsider dynamic keeps many hoping (and praying) that they can ascend the ladder and make up what they are lacking. But the system holds down those who don't measure up and props up those who feed the narcissistic beast. The system seeks to control any dynamic that undermines its effectiveness and longevity. These three factors—structure, shame, and control—are key aspects of narcissistic systems.

And while many ecclesial systems are structured for accountability, those in power often find ways to avoid it. Feedback is not given honestly in a narcissistic system. If it is given, it is tempered, qualified by a long list of strengths and gifts. Loyalty to the narcissistic leader and the system's perpetuation is demanded. It might be said, "This is how we do things" or "This is how we've grown so large." To question this is to express disloyalty and to experience shame and disconnection from the system.

Moreover, when the narcissistic leader is under attack, his response is defensiveness and a victim complex. Narcissistic leaders experience a victim-martyr-hero identity that postures them as the inevitable targets of frustrated subordinates. Their persecution complex actually enhances their status among some who view them as a hero for standing tall amid the battle. The system comes to the rescue of the leader at the expense of his victims. The lack of feedback, fear of disloyalty, and victim complex make it hard to engage, let alone change, this system.

Churches are particularly susceptible to a phenomenon called "collective narcissism," in which the charismatic leader/follower relationship is understood as a given. Sadly, in recent years we've witnessed too many instances of charismatic Christian leaders gaining a massive following, both within the church and on social media, only to be exposed as manipulative, abusive, and dictatorial. Jerrold Post argues that a mutually reinforcing relationship exists between leader and follower.[12] The leader relies on the adoration and respect of his followers; the follower is attracted to the omnipotence and charisma of the leader. The leader uses polarizing rhetoric that identifies an outside enemy, bringing together leader and followers on a grandiose mission. The followers feed off the leader's certainty in order to fill their own empty senses of self. Interestingly, in this mutually reinforcing relationship, both are prone to a form of narcissism.

How can it be that narcissism thrives among those who seek to become like Christ?

First, these systems attract people who want to be a part of something special. The narcissistic system parades its specialness: the unique way God is working mightily in this church or movement or denomination. Who would dare question God's work? Because the mission is tied to God's apparent movement, people are more likely to question their own judgments than God's obvious blessing. However, staff members are often asked to make

large sacrifices for little or no remuneration and are often promised more with little delivery. Those who ascend tend to collude
with the system. Those who ultimately refuse to idealize the
leader are chewed up and spit out. But because the mission is a
seemingly spiritual one, the system goes unchallenged.

Second, the system often compares itself to others and finds
others wanting. The narcissistic system may feature the compelling personality or style of its leader, the strategic nature of its
location or mission, the orthodoxy of its doctrine, the authenticity of its worship, the beauty of its liturgy, the integrity of its
activism. Those within the system are led to believe that the
church down the block isn't as blessed, special, or faithful. A collective sense of grandiosity is common in these situations.

I knew one church in which many of the staff and key leaders
were not theologically trained in a seminary but were equipped
through the lead pastor's own self-created internal program. In
this program, they were led to believe that no church planting
movement had ever experienced more radical or faster growth.
As a result, the church fell into a kind of ecclesial "manifest
destiny." Those who questioned policies, tactics, and even apparent abuses were quickly dismissed. Most, however, believed
they were in an extraordinary place and moment in time, consecrated by God, resulting in criticism of other churches and
even secular organizations that were perceived as less effective
than theirs.

Narcissistic systems exist for themselves, even though their
mission statements and theological beliefs may be filled with the
language of service, selflessness, justice, and care. Those within
the system find this contradiction exhausting. This is why many
who get close to the epicenter of leadership either forfeit their
integrity or resign.

HUMBLE US

The kenosis passage from Philippians 2 presents a vision Christians long to live into but which we sabotage time and again. The cries of "I like Jesus, but I don't like the church" are often borne out of frustrating and even abusive experiences, when the faithful experience shame and humiliation from congregants, leaders, and systems. Pastors and churches lose credibility when instead of embracing the way of Jesus, they go the way of empire, forgoing vulnerability for power and preying on the weak. The narcissistic pastor becomes like the corrupt kings of ancient Israel, whose royal consciousness is marked by power and self-protection rather than solidarity with the wounded sheep. Walter Brueggemann writes,

> In both his teaching and his very presence, Jesus of Nazareth presented the ultimate criticism of the royal consciousness. He has, in fact, dismantled the dominant culture and nullified its claims. The way of his ultimate criticism is his decisive solidarity with marginal people and the accompanying vulnerability required by that solidarity. The only solidarity worth affirming is solidarity characterized by the same helplessness they know and experience.[13]

The long, sordid history of the church testifies to our arrogant love of power, position, wealth, prestige, success, and privilege. As Henri Nouwen says, we long to be relevant, spectacular, and powerful, the toxic cocktail refused by Jesus in his wilderness temptation but gladly embraced by many pastors today.

But given changing ecclesial dynamics and a growing social movement that takes clergy narcissism and abuse seriously, the church and its servants may be in a season of needed humiliation and reckoning. My hope is that we will respond to it humbly.

FURTHER RESOURCES

Walter Brueggemann. *The Prophetic Imagination.* 2nd ed. Minneapolis: Fortress, 2001.

Marva Dawn and Eugene Peterson. *The Unnecessary Pastor: Rediscovering the Call.* Grand Rapids: Eerdmans, 1999.

Henri J. M. Nouwen. *In the Name of Jesus: Reflections on Christian Leadership.* Chestnut Ridge, NY: Crossroad, 1989.

CHAPTER TWO

UNDERSTANDING NARCISSISM

Our godlike beauty is hidden beneath curtains of shame.

GREGORY OF NYSSA

The little boy is terrified. Everyone is looking to him to lead, and he's not sure he can. Tears well up as he folds his arms and starts rocking. *Everyone is looking at me.* His heart races. His jaw clenches. *I hope I don't pass out.* His face burns with a fire that reaches up through his chest and wraps itself around his head, squeezing. *I can't do it. I can't. I'm too scared.*[1]

And then suddenly he declares, "Welcome, friends!" The congregation stands, eager for his leading. *Everyone is looking at me,* he thinks, *and it feels so good.* His heart races. Adrenaline releases like lightning through his tense body. The little boy fades as he commands the stage. "God is good, isn't he?!" he exclaims and hears shouts of "Amen" in response. *They love me,* he thinks.

The little boy or little girl lurks within each of us: our fears, our shame, a deep sense of deficiency. If we are relatively healthy, we befriend our fear, our shame, and our deficiency, and slowly become an integrated person. If not, we flee from these emotions like threatening strangers, living instead from a contingent false self, polished and put together. But while this false self feels the momentary bliss in its detachment from the inner storm, it's really not free at all but stuck on a never-ending hamster wheel, acting out the same script day after day.

The myth of Narcissus tells the story well. While often told as a tale of excessive self-love, it is precisely self-love that Narcissus was lacking. It's a story of being stuck, immobilized, fixed in a death dance. In his youth he ran free, hunting in the forest, loved and desired by young women. But he would let no one touch his heart. This is the wound of shame. One who is ashamed cannot connect and cannot become vulnerable. He is immovable, untouchable.

Narcissus finds himself thirsty one day and makes his way to a clear pool for a drink. In the water he sees his reflection, an image so striking that he reaches in to embrace it. But the image is lost when the water is disrupted, as it is with each future effort, leaving Narcissus all the more desperate. Immobilized before the pool, he pines for the image that will never return his love and eventually succumbs to the neglect of his basic needs.

Terrence Real articulates the tale's meaning well:

> People often think of Narcissus as the symbol of excessive self-regard, but in fact, he exemplifies the opposite. As the Renaissance philosopher Marsilio Ficino observed in the 1500s, Narcissus did not suffer from an overabundance of self-love, but rather from its deficiency. The myth is a parable about paralysis. The youth, who first appears in restless motion, is suddenly rooted to one spot, unable to leave the elusive spirit. As Ficino remarked, if Narcissus had possessed real self-love, he would have been able to leave his fascination. The curse of Narcissus is immobilization, not out of love for himself, but out of dependency upon his image.[2]

Narcissus is trapped in a vicious narcissistic feedback loop. The name *Narcissus* comes from the Greek *narc,* which means numbness—a kind of stupor. It is the sting of addiction that Narcissus experiences. Healthy self-love would have motivated him to befriend every wounded and weary part of himself. Self-contempt motivated him to search in vain for what he thought he needed to live, only to die from a neglect of what he really needed.

But even this story is not without hope, for out of the death of Narcissus emerges a flower. Every redemptive story of one who is narcissistic is a story of death to resurrection.

STUCK IN A MOMENT

Gary is forty-five. I'm his pastor, and he's in my office because his wife, Sherri, intends to leave him if he doesn't begin marital counseling. He shuffles uncomfortably as he tries to convince me that Sherri is a stubborn and needy woman who simply doesn't get men.

"Like last weekend," he says. "A perfect example—I'm hunting with the guys. She expects me to check in every five minutes. What, am I sleeping with whores? Sure, I'm having a few beers, but it's not like I'm doing anything wrong."

When I invite Sherri in, Gary starts grunting and sighing audibly, shifting in his seat, vacillating between a contemptuous gaze at Sherri and a head hung in resignation.

"Sherri, Gary tells me this is all a big misunderstanding. He went hunting, turned off his phone, and you panicked. So, is that your perspective?" My question seems to turn up Sherri's temperature from 98.6 to 400 degrees.

"Chuck, Gary did go hunting. As he has many times on many weekends when his boys have ballgames and Ella has ballet. When he's home, he's in his shop playing with his guns. Or playing video games. Gary is thirteen years old. And unless he grows up, I'm done."

Gary snaps back, "Yeah, thanks Mom, always scolding me. Why would I wanna be around for that?"

If narcissism were a story of self-love, then the cure might be greater selflessness on Gary's part. I might prescribe date nights and acts of service and some flowers, on occasion, as many self-help books do. But Gary doesn't love himself too much. Gary's entitlement, his lack of empathy, his pattern of grandiosity in their relationship—all of these hint at narcissism. And narcissism is born in the soil of shame and self-contempt, not healthy self-love.

Narcissism is not fundamentally about self-love but about an escape from love. The fragile little boy goes into hiding and the protective false self takes the lead. John Bradshaw writes,

> Because the exposure of self to self lies at the heart of neu-
> rotic shame, escape from the self is necessary. The escape
> from self is accomplished by creating a false self. The false
> self is always more or less than human. The false self may be
> a perfectionist or a slob, a family Hero or a family Scapegoat.
> As the false self is formed, the authentic self goes into hiding.
> Years later the layers of defense and pretense are so intense
> that one loses all conscious awareness of who one really is.[3]

But the false self isn't an adult. It's a child, stuck in adolescence, perpetually replaying outdated ways of getting its needs met in its present, adult body. Like Narcissus, it looks and looks, only to become more isolated, more turned in on itself.[4] It may love the image it has created, but it has no real capacity to love itself.

Amy led a ministry that reached tens of thousands of people in need, but she was radically out of touch with her own needs. In truth, Amy's own ego was bolstered by the large staff and significant impact her organization had. The staff and organization were an extension of her own identity, the pool in which her image was reflected. So when the organization was audited and its financial integrity was called into question, she decompensated. A usually strong and resilient leader, Amy fell apart on the floor of my office, writhing around, moaning, and wailing.

When we analyzed the experience later, Amy reported that she felt about three or four years old during her cathartic episode. She said, "It was like there was trauma stuck in my body that had never been released."[5] I assigned her to watch Disney's *The Kid*, starring Bruce Willis in an unlikely role. She seemed perplexed but followed through. Several days later, she sent an email saying, "*The Kid* destroyed me."

In *The Kid*, Bruce Willis plays Russ Duritz, an image consultant—an appropriate role for a narcissist. Hardworking and demanding, Russ lives through his work and his wealth, and defines his success by it. But it comes at a cost, rendering him cold and unempathetic, and distancing him from key relationships, not least his father. Then he meets a strange child named Rusty. Puzzled by Rusty's seemingly random appearances, he determines to track him down, only to be led on a journey into his own past. In time, it becomes clear that Rusty is Russ at a younger age. Russ bears witness to an encounter with his father he'd long forgotten, a painful moment in which he is blamed for adding stress to his ill mother. Amidst tears, his father forcefully shakes and scolds him, wiping away his tears and telling him to grow up. A facial tick would be the only external mark of this incident in Russ's present experience, but an inner posture of control, defensiveness, and achievement would leave even more indelible scars.

"I see what you were trying to do," said Amy when I saw her next. Through tears, she told me of being an only child, aware at around age three or four of her father's rage and her mother's fear. She began to recall how she'd become responsible for her mother's care, lifting her mother's spirits with humor and charm. But Amy had never grieved her own terror and shame. It didn't take much longer for her to begin connecting the dots, recognizing that she'd become the caretaker for literally thousands of others while neglecting her own care.

Narcissism may not sound like an appropriate description for Amy, be as she made sense of her story it was the only word she could settle on. She'd become grandiose, entitled, a Savior figure to staff and those she helped. Yet many experienced her as cold, distant, and unempathetic, and 360-degree assessments showed patterns of condescension and staff fatigue around Amy's demands.

"My father was a narcissist," she said. "I've always known it. I just became a more sanctified version of him. I've been stuck in that trauma for thirty-five years, and it took a bad audit for me to see it and to face myself."

DEFINING NARCISSISM

Narcissism moved from myth to science in the late nineteenth century, when a British sexologist named Havelock Ellis described a "Narcissus-like" complex in which people satisfied themselves sexually. But it wasn't until 1914 that Sigmund Freud put narcissism on the map in his essay *On Narcissism*. Freud saw narcissistic egocentricity as a necessary stage of growth but problematic if it continued into adulthood. Interestingly, competing views of healthy versus unhealthy narcissism became the subject of debate, but the work of the aforementioned Christopher Lasch, dependent in large part on psychologist Otto Kernberg's more cynical view of narcissism, became the dominant chord in the debate. Today many argue that the binary, either/or caricature of narcissism isn't helpful because it ignores healthy aspects of growth in confidence and self-esteem.[6]

Today the criteria for narcissistic personality disorder (NPD) is found in the *Diagnostic and Statistical Manual* of the American Psychiatric Association, updated with key revisions in June 2011. For better or for worse, this is the industry standard, debated every several years by professionals who deliberate until they find some consensus. In the last update, there was an interesting debate about whether or not NPD should be a category on its own or an overarching cluster of disorders, including the so-called "Cluster-B" disorders, including borderline personality disorder (BPD), histrionic personality disorder (HPD), and antisocial personality disorder (APD). My own experience says that while there are essential features of NPD, there is a variance of experience best imagined through multiple lenses, like the nine I'll present in the next chapter. In other words, there isn't a single caricature of narcissism—it comes in many faces.

The *DSM-V* offers a comprehensive set of criteria to define narcissism:

A. Significant impairments in personality functioning manifest by:

1. Impairments in self functioning (a or b):

a. *Identity*: Excessive reference to others for self-definition and self-esteem regulation; exaggerated self-appraisal may be inflated or deflated, or vacillate between extremes; emotional regulation mirrors fluctuations in self-esteem.

b. *Self-direction*: Goal-setting is based on gaining approval from others; personal standards are unreasonably high in order to see oneself as exceptional, or too low based on a sense of entitlement; often unaware of own motivations.

AND

    2. Impairments in interpersonal functioning (a or b):

        a. *Empathy:* Impaired ability to recognize or identify with the feelings and needs of others; excessively attuned to reactions of others, but only if perceived as relevant to self; over- or underestimate of own effect on others.

        b. *Intimacy:* Relationships largely superficial and exist to serve self-esteem regulation; mutuality constrained by little genuine interest in others experiences and predominance of a need for personal gain.

B. Pathological personality traits in the following domain:

    1. Antagonism, characterized by:

        a. *Grandiosity:* Feelings of entitlement, either overt or covert; self-centeredness; firmly holding to the belief that one is better than others; condescending toward others.

        b. *Attention seeking:* Excessive attempts to attract and be the focus of the attention of others; admiration seeking.

C. The impairments in personality functioning and the individual's personality trait expression are relatively stable across time and consistent across situations.

D. The impairments in personality functioning and the individual's personality trait expression are not better understood as normative for the individual's developmental stage or sociocultural environment.

E. The impairments in personality functioning and the individual's personality trait expression are not solely due to the direct physiological effects of a substance (e.g., a drug of abuse, medication) or a general medical condition (e.g., severe head trauma).[7]

You might agree with me that there's a lot in this definition. Allow me to highlight a few key characteristics.

First, you'll see that grandiosity and attention seeking are grouped under just one aspect of a larger set of criteria. These are often the first things we think about when we consider narcissism, but there is always much more at work.

Second, note the impairments of empathy or intimacy. The narcissist is always out of touch with himself and others. While he may be charming or ingratiating, this personality is a false self, which protects the true self from shame and exposure. Often people will talk about being drawn into the orbit of a narcissist but note how difficult it is to connect to him once they are in the orbit. In a ministry context, this can be especially dangerous, as those called to pastor, teach, or care for others have a heightened ability to feign empathy. This is a skill learned early in life amid the original wounds of childhood, a defensive and self-protective mechanism that allows for relationship without the risk of real vulnerability.

Third, notice how out of touch the narcissist is with his sense of identity and direction. This does not mean the narcissistic person is vocationally unsuccessful, but that he is out of touch with his deepest self, finding his identity in the pool that best reflects back what he wants to see. In ministry, pastors use their congregations to validate a sense of identity and worth. The church becomes an extension of the narcissistic ego, and its ups and downs lead to seasons of ego inflation and ego deflation for the pastor. Today social media platforms add to this mix. Because his sense of identity is bound up in external realities, his sense of mission is wavering and unmoored, often manifesting in constantly shifting visions and programs, frequent dissatisfaction with the status quo, and anxious engagement with staff and members.

THE NARCISSISTIC SPECTRUM

The *DSM-V* doesn't say everything that needs to be said about narcissism. Indeed, narcissism comes in many different faces and forms, some that look like classic caricatures and others that are subtler and sometimes even more insidious.

For starters, it is important to remember that narcissism exists along a spectrum from healthy to toxic (see figure 2.1).[8] On one end is a healthy narcissism, where we live humbly yet confidently, anchored by an experience of being loved deeply at a core level. Picture a child who boldly performs a cartwheel for her father, receiving his delight. When we're loved well, we develop a healthy and holy confidence. Where we see healthy narcissism, we'll also notice a healthy shame, a recognition of our limitations and a humble acknowledgment that we're not the center of the world. Note how both work in tandem. Translated for Christians, this is an acknowledgment of both our beauty and brokenness, a recognition of God's delight in us alongside a recognition of our human weakness and fragility. Both are essential for a wholehearted life in Christ.

Healthy narcissism, both personally and organizationally, manifests in confidence rather than certainty, empathy rather than ingratiation, clarity rather than confusion, humility rather than arrogance, curiosity rather than defensiveness.[9] Over the years, I've met many gifted pastors, for instance, whose public persona might be construed as narcissistic because of their confidence and charisma, but whose humility and self-understanding demonstrate health instead of pathology. This is why it is mostly unhelpful to toss labels around based on appearances. Clinicians have the tools and capacity for assessment that laypeople do not have.

Some people show elevations on the narcissistic spectrum that indicate a narcissistic *style* of relating.[10] This is not alarming in itself. Indeed, one may manifest the characteristics of health we

Figure 2.1. The narcissism spectrum

just looked at. At times, there are circumstantial reasons for the elevation—a particularly challenging season of ministry leading to ego-defensiveness, for instance. Or the elevation may be representative of a long-time pattern of relating that masks some shame-based insecurity or anxiety, but which the person is aware of and capable of navigating. A style is not a pathology, but as a clinician I want to pay close attention to how it plays out in a person's life and what animates it from within.

An even more pronounced elevation is the narcissistic *type*. In this case, a narcissistic personality is more defined and potentially more of a problem. These are folks that an average onlooker might describe as narcissistic based on classic caricatures of narcissism. Indeed, these elevations may indicate the presence of toxic shame and a coping pattern that protects and defends from further shame. However, in my experience, those in the range of *style* to *type* have the capacity for some measure of curiosity. Though perhaps defensive at first, they may relax their guard to assess their inner world and engage honestly in hard conversations about the implications of their narcissism. I see this at times in my pastoral candidate assessments, as a conversation about narcissistic elevations leads to honest self-reflection and candid confessions of the potential impact of their behavior. That said, the more elevated someone is, the more pronounced the narcissistic behavior may be, leading to potential issues in relationships, work, and other aspects of life.

As we reach the latter end of the spectrum, we find a patho-logical narcissism that is diagnosable and often toxic in relation-ships and the workplace. Here the psyche is hijacked by a "false self" that becomes the primary mask the narcissist wears in the world.[11] The narcissistic person becomes convinced that this is who he is, and the cost of his loss of connection to his core true self manifests in a toxic style of relating. Sadly, when narcissism becomes toxic, the person generally has little to no capacity to see herself or see the debris of relational damage in her wake. Her ego-defensiveness is the product of years of self-protection. And most clinicians would be skeptical about the prospect of substantial change.

GRANDIOSE AND VULNERABLE NARCISSISM

Sometimes people come to me perplexed by what they perceive to be egocentric and narcissistic behavior, but they're puzzled because it does not come in the usually grandiose package. I find the distinction between grandiose and vulnerable narcissism help-ful.[12] These are probably best understood as two sides of a coin rather than two distinct variations. "Grandiose narcissism" looks like the classic definition of narcissism, including the typical gran-diosity, lack of empathy, and identity and intimacy impairments. "Vulnerable narcissism" looks more fragile, hypervigilant, shy, sen-sitive, and depressed. Clinicians are more likely to find the vulner-able narcissistic state when life isn't working as intended. When the grandiose posture cannot be maintained and relationships or work are impacted, "he or she is more and more vulnerable to shame, panic, helplessness or depression as life progresses with-out support from admiring others."[13]

Closely related to this are expressions of overt and covert nar-cissism. While there are popular articles and blogs that make this distinction,[14] these are expressions of grandiose and vulnerable narcissism rather than separate categories.[15] Overt expressions include behaviors, expressed attitudes, and emotions more visible to others. Covert expressions include cognitions, private feelings, secret motives, and deeper needs that are likely hidden and often unknown even to oneself.

These and other helpful categorizations provide us with a bigger and broader picture of narcissism beyond the classic caricature.[16] Knowing them can help you understand why you feel a bit crazy or manipulated or just confused at times in relationship with someone whose personality style is difficult but may not appear classically narcissistic. These distinctions may also help caution us from dropping the word irresponsibly on social media or in casual conversation.[17]

WHAT A CLUSTER

A church planting assessment committee I was working with was stunned when a candidate did not test as narcissistic but instead showed the highest elevations possible on another spectrum altogether—histrionic personality disorder (HPD). The chairman asked, "He's not narcissistic, then?" It's a complicated question, and worth exploring.

As it turns out, NPD shares the characteristics of problematic emotional regulation and impulse control with its closest *DSM-V* cousins, which all find a home in what the *DSM-V* calls "Cluster B Personality Disorders." My clinical contention is that each of the personality disorders within this cluster has NPD at its base but shows unique features not seen in NPD proper. This is why there are different "faces" of narcissism.

In my own work, I see HPD show up as an elevation frequently when I assess pastors, pastoral candidates, and Christian ministry leaders. HPD presents with less grandiosity than NPD, but its characteristic feature is attention seeking. Those on the HPD spectrum long for the attention and approval of others, and they use their words or appearance or actions to grab the attention they seek so desperately. This is a person who is always on stage, whose characteristic flair for the dramatic may show up in ways that inspire but also offend. They often have shallow relationships and tend to overestimate intimacy, believing certain friendships are deeper and more honest than they really are. Relational closeness may fluctuate based on the usefulness of the person for his agenda. Further, many with HPD will be drawn to the latest and most relevant products or strategies or fads which can lead to confusion and constant change in a ministry setting. HPD pastors can be adrenaline and adventure junkies, alcohol and nicotine addicts, and big spenders. I often hear them claim ADD or ADHD as a way of excusing their behaviors. They may overshare emotionally and dramatically but shun real vulnerability or connection. In the end, this cousin of narcissism shares many of narcissism's traits and can bite just as hard.

Though I do not see it as frequently among pastors, another cousin sometimes makes an appearance—borderline personality disorder (BPD). BPD features an interpersonal instability that makes consistent, healthy relating difficult. People with BPD may have dramatic personas that are appealing, but their need for constant reassurance and pervasive fear of abandonment may be wearying to those around them. They may lash out in rage at others or harm themselves. Ultimately, an inner sense of emptiness and shame is pervasive. Their narcissism manifests as less grandiose and more vulnerable, characterized by insecurity, shame, and fear. Because of the interpersonal demands of pastoral ministry, my belief is that those with diagnosable BPD cannot and will not last long in a visible pastoral role and will find other outlets for ministry like counseling or chaplaincy. That said, pastors will often encounter women and men with BPD in their congregations and will often find caring for them to be especially challenging.[18] Finally, antisocial personality disorder (APD), sometimes called sociopathy, is deeply alarming and painful when it shows up in ecclesial and ministry settings. Indeed, though the *DSM-V* has not yet recognized it as an official, clinical category, some theorists have chosen the term "malignant narcissism" to describe the narcissist with sociopathic behaviors.[19] Prone to callous indifference, manipulation, and rule breaking, APD shows up often among pastoral predators who use and abuse their power to exploit others. Those with APD appear shameless. They often act with a belief that they won't be caught, or that they are above accountability or consequences. An even more pronounced narcissism, APD may appear arrogant yet charming, manipulative yet convincing, exciting yet dangerous. Those drawn into the gravitational field of someone with APD are often highly susceptible to their powerful, confident, and seemingly infallible persona. But the relational debris they leave behind them may be their ultimate downfall.

LOOKING BENEATH THE WATERLINE

While diagnostic definitions are helpful, they do not reveal the mammoth iceberg of shame that hides beneath the surface and that drives narcissistic behavior. Indeed, it's only when we see below the waterline that we begin to understand and have empathy for a narcissist.

Shame drives narcissism. It's the age-old story. The early church theologian St. Gregory of Nyssa said our "godlike beauty" is "hidden beneath curtains of shame."[20] And while theologians have often named pride as the reason for humanity's fall from grace illustrated in Genesis 3, it is more compelling—both theologically and psychologically—to see shame as the underlying force that propelled Adam and Eve toward the forbidden tree. The serpent, like a fine-tuned inner critic, appeals to their lack. Adam and Eve think they have been deprived. Given an extraordinary garden, they are forbidden from partaking from a particular tree—the tree of the knowledge of good and evil. Is God holding out on them? Adam and Eve experience limitation for the first time. Why do Adam and Eve reach for the fruit? Perhaps they've already begun to believe the lie of toxic shame—that it's not enough, that they're not enough, and perhaps most important, they've started to doubt God's goodness as well.

All addictions begin in shame. They don't begin with troubling behavior—a binge on porn, a night of overdrinking—but with a sense of lack or limitation.[21] An addict may be loved deeply, but like Narcissus he is blind to it, trapped in a desperate cycle of attempted self-salvation. Adam and Eve had everything, but they perceived that something was missing and then took satisfaction into their own hands rather than embracing their creaturely, God-given limits.

I was speaking on shame a couple of years ago when someone in the audience shouted out, "I get it, but we're living in a shameless culture. People don't feel shame anymore. They do whatever they want." I hear the lament in this, but there is more to the story. While the prevalent thinking has been that Western societies tend to suppress shame, sociologist Thomas Scheff's research shows that the threshold of shame in Western societies is actually decreasing.[22] We are more likely both to experience it and, at the same time, to suppress it.

This is a frightening finding. We are most prone to act out when we are out of touch with our shame, unaware of our limitations, unfamiliar with the deep questions lurking beneath the waterline. Unfamiliar with or uneasy about our inner emptiness, sadness, or shame, we're apt to displace it onto food or drink, sex or drugs, even people. We're out of touch with ourselves, our hearts, our story, our feelings. We walk the earth using others and using things to satisfy the deep ache within. In doing so, we leave behind debris fields of pain, broken relationships, and shattered dreams. Shame is fundamentally about an inner disconnection, arising from our childhoods, that leads to relational disconnection in the present.[23] In the absence of real connection and intimacy, we search for a substitute. We use and manipulate people, food, substances, even spirituality, in a search for the inner completion we long for.[24] At its most extreme, narcissism can manifest in violence, bullying, coercion, and lawlessness. All the while, a massive iceberg of shame is driving it.

Few know that this is the inner drama of one who suffers from narcissism. Few can empathize with their desperate need to connect to something—anything—when narcissism's bite penetrates and wounds. And yet, only by tending to the inner wound can one truly heal from it. The little boy or girl within is wounded, and the well-crafted narcissistic false self provides a shield to protect the child. But the child longs to be known. And I'm convinced, based on my work with narcissists, that the protective false self is weary and longs to be done with the charade.

That said, as I'm regularly reminded in my work with those who've been abused by narcissists, the narcissist's story of woundedness is never, ever an excuse for their abuse. Narcissists are not above using their story or perceived victim status as an excuse and a means to manipulate. Those who are drawn into the gravitational pull of narcissism may even enable the narcissist by letting him off the hook for his behavior. We look beneath the waterline as a means of understanding, even empathizing, but never excusing narcissistic behavior—particularly in its most abusive forms.

But we need to recognize the complex psychological dynamics at work in the narcissist. In doing so, we're equipped for awareness, self-protection, and—with wisdom and discernment—empathy.

FURTHER RESOURCES

John Bradshaw. *Healing the Shame That Binds You*. Deerfield Beach, FL: Health Communications, 2005.

W. Keith Campbell and Joshua D. Miller, eds. *The Handbook of Narcissism and Narcissistic Personality Disorder: Theoretical Approaches, Empirical Findings, and Treatments*. Hoboken, NJ: Wiley and Sons, 2011.

James Masterson. *Search for the Real Self: Unmasking the Personality Disorders of Our Age*. New York: Free Press, 1988.

CHAPTER THREE

THE NINE FACES OF NARCISSISM

Take off your mask. Your face is glorious.

RUMI

Because many tend to associate narcissism with the grandiose politician or the megachurch pastor, it's crucial that we expand our perspective, paying particular attention to the broader range of narcissism we see in our daily lives and in the church. In this chapter, I want to put flesh on the bones of theory, offering profiles of nine faces of narcissism.

The nine faces are my unique application of an important tool called the Enneagram. This tool helps us identify our masks or *personas*—the false selves that hide our true selves and sabotage love of self, God, and neighbor. Thomas Merton warns us of the implications of mistaking our mask for our true face:

> Now if we take our vulnerable shell to be our true identity, if we think our mask is our true face, we will protect it with fabrications even at the cost of violating our own truth. This seems to be the collective endeavor of society: the more busily men dedicate themselves to it, the more certainly it becomes a collective illusion, until in the end we have the enormous, obsessive uncontrollable dynamic of fabrication

designed to protect mere fictitious identities—"selves," that is to say, regarded as objects.[1]

The Enneagram helps free us from our illusions and fabrications, inviting us to embrace our deepest, truest self in Christ. An early Enneagram sage named Oscar Ichazo called the faces "fixations"— ways in which we become fixed, attached, even addicted to ways of living life apart from the ever-abundant grace of God. The language of fixation resonates with the narrative of narcissism, that idea that we become fixed on our false self, immobilized, and numbed to aliveness and presence in the world.

Unlike many contemporary personality assessments, the Enneagram identifies disordered patterns and habits of relating emerging from our prewired personality plus our childhood wounds.[2] In time, this personality is recognized as fixed—who we are—though that is not at all to say that our flawed ways of relating can't be changed. The Enneagram is uninhibited in its use of the language of sin, recognizing an important insight: that sin is not fundamentally about a bad behavior we do, but about habits that become ingrained as we attempt to get primitive needs met. Sin is how we live outside of union with God, who dwells within us (1 Corinthians 3:16) but whose presence we can evade and avoid through self-sabotaging patterns of living.

The early church fathers named the primary sin patterns "passions," borrowing a Latin term that could also be translated "sufferings." As we live out a unique pattern or "face" of sin, we begin to think the face is our own. Theologian Wendy Farley writes, "Passions become second nature and seem to be an essential part of our identity. The more they have entwined themselves with one's self-identity, the more difficult they will be to dethrone."[3] The Enneagram identifies nine passions: nine ways our God-given selves can be eclipsed by a false self, with an energy driving it toward self-satisfaction and shame reduction rather than deep fulfillment in God's shalom. As you read, be open to patterns that may have emerged a long time ago in you or in someone you love, patterns that do not represent the true self but have become a mask, a face you wear to weather the storms of life.

The Enneagram is organized around three triads, primary energy centers that are represented as heart types, head types, and gut/body types. In this chapter, we'll use this organizational schema, looking first at the heart types (Two, Three, and Four), then the head types (Five, Six, and Seven), and finally the gut/body types (Eight, Nine, and One). Heart types are primarily shame based, head types are primarily anxiety based, and gut/body types are primarily anger based.[4] Interestingly, the major psychoanalytic debates about NPD might be summarized as debates around what lies at the core of narcissism—narcissistic rage/anger, primitive shame, or chronic anxiety.[5] This is not mere coincidence, but a psychoanalytic attempt to take the data of people's experiences seriously. The Enneagram triads may be a way of explaining these differing theories.

The three major energy centers of heart, head, and gut/body are like three potential pathways we may take based on a unique interplay of nature and nurture in stories. Thomas Keating explains that as a result of our childhood wounds, we seek to meet our needs through the pathways of esteem and affection (heart types), security and survival (head types), and power and control (gut/body types).[6] The further expansion of these energy centers into three distinct types paints an even more diverse picture of how narcissism can manifest. This keeps us from defaulting to one monolithic caricature of narcissism while showing how unique features of NPD may be more on display in one personality than another.

At the end of the chapter, I'll provide resources for further exploration of the Enneagram, so if this is new language for you, there's no need to panic. I also include an appendix at the end of the book with thoughts on growth and transformation for each type.

To my knowledge, no one has made a clear connection between the Enneagram and personality disorders before. However, having worked with and taught the Enneagram for more than fifteen years, I think the connections I make are worthwhile and helpful additions to conversations on both narcissism and the Enneagram.[7] With each type, I try not to present a merely toxic form of narcissism but hope that the reader can discern the fine line between the gift healthy narcissism can be and the bite it can inflict when toxic.

I invite you to read these descriptions slowly and deliberately, not with an eye toward a quick means to pigeonhole another person, but with a humility that recognizes that each of us, regardless of whether we're on the narcissistic spectrum or not, is both beautiful and broken, complex and unique.

THE HEART TYPES (SHAME)

Type Two: The savior. The church is perhaps the arena in which overfunctioning happens the most. Marva Dawn and Eugene Peterson write, "The constant danger for those of us who enter the ranks of the ordained is that we take on a role, a professional religious role, that gradually obliterates the life of the soul.... Humility recedes as leadership advances."[8] Because we view our tasks as holy and sacred, we go above and beyond to help, to please, to serve. Sometimes, we tie our very worth to our capacity to give. This can be especially true among clergy, who show high rates of compassion fatigue and burnout.[9]

Exhaustion and resentment are the burdens of what author and therapist Michael Cusick calls the "benevolent narcissist."[10] Though motivated to help, the driving force may not be empathy but ego, prone to fix her own wounds by trying to fix others. She may appear engaging, available, and selfless, but there is a secret scheming going on behind the scenes, all in service of her own need to control her own pain by controlling others.

Jan was an only child, born to parents whose academic credentials and scholarly contributions were unassailable. Jan's arrival in the world was celebrated at first, but it did not take long for her mother (Debra) to recognize that Jan was an interruption to her professional life. Debra struggled to bond with Jan, finding herself resentful at times and regretful at others. Sadly, Jan internalized at a very early age that her neediness pushed Mommy away, and in time she became compliant, cheerful, and helpful. Jan was commended for being the "big girl" or "Mommy's helper" and was sometimes given the responsibility of gathering Mommy's books or entertaining her colleagues. She could make everyone feel good about themselves. She learned how to work a room. Soon enough she was enrolled in a competitive and elite Christian academy and was told that she'd change the world someday. Everything about her early life became geared to pleasing, charming, helping, saving the day, and saving the world.

Fast forward to Jan at forty. She's exhausted. Her sense of self-importance has caught up with her. Always there, always helpful, always responsible, always charming, she's become bitter and resentful. Now a pastor, she's angry at a congregation she feels does not serve enough or give enough financially. In truth, her overfunctioning leaves little room for their participation. Her frustration and resentment come out in manipulative guilt trips in sermons, condescending dialogue, and passive-aggressive social media posts. Her people feel confused—she's always quick to show up in a crisis, perpetually charming and seemingly invulnerable, always going above and beyond, yet they feel later as if they owe her something.

Those in the orbit of this benevolently narcissistic person may feel confused, since a mixed message is always projected: "I can do it all" *and* "you never do enough." When others do not come through for her, she grows resentful and angry, quietly judging the other. Seething with resentment but unwilling to admit it, she ignores her own needs. Cut off from her heart, she becomes hard-hearted, and in so doing may become cruel, manipulative, aggressive, and vindictive.

Type Three: The winner. Smartly dressed and slick as a car salesman, Jake sauntered back and forth on stage, delivering his sermon to perfection. The congregation took notes. "Amens" were loud and frequent. Jake's smile seemed to reach from one side of the stage to the other.

When you are in relationship with this person, he's the winner and you feel like a loser. He knows how to close the deal while you're just a scared and insecure loafer. All of your middle school insecurities about not being as cool as the cheerleader or point guard emerge. You feel less-than, incomplete, incompetent, not good enough.

This face of narcissism often looks like the classic caricature of *grandiose* narcissism—the charming, superior, exceptional person. They have an almost desperate need to be seen. The thrill of accomplishment is like a dopamine-high, leading to an addictive need for more. Workaholism is a common feature, but often they ascend to positions of leadership, demanding the same drivenness from others. Out of touch with their inner feelings and needs, they remain at the emotional surface, often incapable of empathy or real connection. Yet they feed off applause and affection. They live for the win. Perhaps more importantly, they are terrified of failure. When feelings of failure are triggered, there can be a Jekyll-and-Hyde effect that flips the switch from charm to rage. The sometimes slick-talking salesman can become belligerent, using his verbal abilities to insult, to manipulate, to demean, to condescend. Feelings of failure are projected onto the other in order to protect the fragile ego. The great twentieth-century psychologist Heinz Kohut called this "narcissistic rage," a defensive protection against shame.[11] What is often tricky in the church is that people don't see the dark side. A spouse experiencing abuse may be questioned when the abuser is charming, winsome, and convincing. How could *he* be abusive?

In their book *The Faces of Forgiveness*, theologian F. LeRon Shults and psychologist Steven J. Sandage write that "the narcissistic tendencies toward exploitiveness and entitlement reflect a desire to use power against others and a sense of deserving excessive admiration and respect."[12] These are traits and tendencies that do not belong in a follower of Jesus, and yet in ministry settings narcissistic leaders can corral great power and may wield their power in cruel, manipulative, devious, and exploitative ways. Indeed, their rage is often accompanied by a simmering jealousy of anyone who steals attention, power, or admiration from them.

Jake's church plant grew over a decade into a two-thousand-member-plus, multisite church, but with growth Jake's drive didn't ease. He grew more powerful and more suspicious of anyone who threatened his power, and his unending need to be the center of attention led him to undermine, exasperate, and even terminate his best staff members over the years. His adoring fan base loved his many books on God's love and grace, but those in his closest orbit experienced his wrath. His addictive need for admiration led to several emotional affairs and an eventual physical affair, which loyal admirers helped him cover up.

Merton writes, "Pride makes us artificial and humility makes us real."[13] The hope is that a person like this will experience failure and humiliation and learn from it. The sad reality is that many try to cover up failure and protect against anything that might dull the shiny veneer.

Type Four: The individualist. We all long to be special to someone, but the Enneagram Four has a profound longing to be seen, understood, and regarded as particularly unique and special. There is an inner ache, a sense of incompleteness, an ever-present, quietly humming sadness within. As is the case with the entire heart energy center, shame is the quiet driver behind the scenes.

The capacity to feel deeply is simultaneously the great gift and the great burden of this person. Prone to a more vulnerable form of narcissism, the pain is introverted, manifesting in a sense of never being enough, emerging at times in feelings of self-pity and despair. You may experience a storm of drama in this person's life, propelled by unmet needs that flash out of the storm's center like darts, piercing the one who misses or misunderstands her. Though capable of great emotion, she may be less capable of empathy because she tends primarily to her own pain. Her relationships can be intense, fiery, and passionate, but they are up and down. At one moment, you're in, you're loved, you're a confidant; at another, you've betrayed her. An assessment of this person may reveal a diagnosis like histrionic or borderline personality disorder, but the narcissistic impact is no less.

Becca's compelling personality and fashion sense caused heads to turn in high school and college. But now she finds herself in her first job doing youth ministry at a large church, often working long hours and feeling unnoticed by the lead youth pastor and unappreciated by the kids. Rather than tending to her pain, she harms herself by cutting. Somehow the act of methodically carving lines into her forearm both numbs the deeper pain and gives her a sense of control. Her increasing pain leads to self-sabotage at work too. A male coworker's promotion enrages her, and she unwisely sends out a reactive email to the entire church staff. No one knows how to engage her; they experience her like a ticking time bomb. Quietly, the murmurs are consistent: "It's always about Becca."

Becca's vulnerable narcissism actually covers her lifelong shame. She wants to be seen, loved, and understood but sabotages this need with attention-getting drama and victimization. Paradoxically, the people who love her value her unique personality, but they don't know how to care for her and feel confused about whether they're in or out. Consequently, colleagues at church do a relational dance when they're around her, trying to decide whether to engage or avoid her.

The intense longing of this person manifests in envy, an ever-present sense that someone has that missing thing that I need. Even more, those with this energy feel entitled to that illusive thing. For people in relationship with Becca, this can be confusing and exasperating; at worst, it may be experienced as abusive and crazy-making. The chaos she projects outwardly, however, is a projection of the chaos she feels within.

HEAD TYPES (ANXIETY)

Type Five: The distancer. As the pastor facilitates their pastoral counseling session, Jennifer shares honestly from her heart while her husband Gary takes notes on a yellow legal pad, occasionally raising his hand to his chin in order to think about what to write next. Gary is fifty and he's been married to Jennifer for twenty-seven years. She reports that she's tired of being married to a computer. "All he does is information input and output. It's like he is incapable of empathy or emotion." Gary, a seminary biblical languages professor and author of several textbooks, looks condescendingly at Jennifer if he does make eye contact.

This is narcissism as intellectual elitism. He knows better than you. He is distant, seemingly unemotional, and prides himself on not feeling. You are needy and too emotional. He has it all figured out and you're a mess. Grandiosity in this person is experienced in his distant, preoccupied disposition, which can come across as superior and condescending. Receding into the control tower of his mind, he watches you and others from a distance, evaluating, analyzing, gathering data, all which may be used against you when the time is right.

Often these are women and men who were gifted at an early age. Many were early readers, content to be alone for hours with a book rather than engaging with peers. But those who become narcissistic experienced shame early in life. Perhaps they felt like they knew better or more than a parent. Perhaps their social isolation was criticized. Perhaps abuse drove them into an inner sanctum. Regardless, those within their orbit feel less smart, less thoughtful, less informed. In her bestselling *The Drama of the Gifted Child*, Alice Miller describes them as

> people who, as children, were intellectually far beyond their parents and therefore admired by them, but who also therefore had to solve their own problems alone. These people, who give us a feeling of their intellectual strength and will power, also seem to demand that we, too, ought to fight off any feeling of weakness with intellectual means. In their presence one feels one cannot be recognized as a person with problems just

as they and their problems were unrecognized by their parents, for whom he always had to be strong.[14]

The church can have a unique draw for those with special knowledge. Gnosticism has always occupied a special place in ecclesiastical history, and certain denominations and traditions tend to privilege intellectualism.

In my early years, my father followed a Christian radio personality whose Bible studies and question-and-answer sessions featured eccentric allegorical and spiritualized interpretations of Scripture. While his multiple predictions of the end of the world never came to pass, many followed him, and some made major life decisions based on his fringe theories. He was enlightened—or so many thought.

Interestingly, I suspect that my father and I—both susceptible to shame and insecurity—fed off of this leader's intellectual certainty. We both awakened to this in due time, in large part because the enlightened one, though sometimes impressive, often proved himself incapable of mature, nuanced thinking and relating. His intellectual intelligence was unaccompanied by emotional intelligence.

With someone manifesting this kind of narcissistic energy, it can take years to get in touch, at an emotional level, with feelings of loss and shame. More often than not, it takes seeing the impact he has on those closest to him—like a child who is dejected because he is so aloof—for him to feel the loss he experienced as a child. The hope is that he might experience a taste of humility and relational curiosity. As the great desert father Evagrius Ponticus said, "Blessed is the one who has arrived at infinite ignorance."[15]

Type Six: The hawkeye. The baseline anxiety of one who is hypervigilantly narcissistic can be exhausting. Often overly sensitive, fearful, and rule conscious, this person is the hawkeye,

always on alert. They are often drawn to the church because of a
need to experience boundaries, moral regulations, and certainty.
They prefer consistency and become suspicious in situations
where there is unpredictability or spontaneity.

Sandra's years of leadership at Ebenezer Baptist saw many
storms, but she prided herself in being the steady anchor, always
quick to remind people of what the church had always done and
stood for. She could see a crisis from a mile away and put out the
fire. As chair of the pastoral search committee for almost twenty
years, she had the strongest hand in choosing the pastor. She'd
always manage to find a "steady Eddie," as she'd call him—a faithful, dutiful pastor who'd preach the Word and keep the tradition
of Ebenezer alive.

However, she wasn't on the committee when Howard was
selected. Howard had a vision for change, and Sandra could smell
it from his first sermon. Within weeks, she was feeding doubt
about Howard's leadership into the minds of her friends. When
Howard proposed "modernizing the worship service," she couldn't
contain herself. She launched into him during an elder meeting,
shouting at him about violating the traditions of the church and
calling for his resignation. Yet no one took her side. It was Roxie,
a fellow elder who'd served alongside Sandra for a decade, who
finally had the courage to say, "We've walked on eggshells around
you for years, and I can't do it anymore. Things are going to
change, and you'll need to face your control issues."

Gabbard writes that hypervigilant narcissists "listen to others
carefully for evidence of any critical reaction, and they tend to feel
slighted at every turn."[16] At their core, they fear rejection, so they
seek to control their reality in order to prevent it. Noting the characteristics of growing unhealth in this person, Don Richard Riso and
Russ Hudson of the Enneagram Institute explain, "To compensate

for insecurities, they become sarcastic and belligerent, blaming others for their problems, taking a tough stance toward 'outsiders.' Highly reactive and defensive, dividing people into friends and enemies, while looking for threats to their own security. Authoritarian while fearful of authority, highly suspicious, yet, conspiratorial, and fear-instilling to silence their own fears."[17]

Hypervigilant narcissists create anxiety in the people and systems around them. Out of a sense of principle or duty, they can hijack good processes and plans, stuck in worry and fearful of change. They are guardians of systems and ideas, and any threat feels like a move toward chaos, descending into anarchy. The narcissistic pull is experienced as more vulnerable, lacking in grandiosity but high in control, with a lack of empathy and a hijacked identity.

Sadly, those who struggle with hypervigilance will often admit that they lack joy. Fixed and obsessed on the thing they can manage, they lose sight of those who love them and miss out on opportunities for growth and change.

Type Seven: The optimist. Despite his wife's pain, Travis continued to speak about the Lord's goodness and the provision of God. His wife, Shanna, sat quietly, feeling abandoned by God amidst her cancer diagnosis, but he kept reminding her that this was "God's good plan" and that she'd experience healing "right around the corner."

Travis was the eternal optimist, always looking to the new good thing God could do in his life, always planning ahead, cheerful and bright. But Shanna's illness provoked an even greater anxiety in him, sending him into a frenzy of spiritual platitudes that only repulsed Shanna. "I don't need your spiritualizing, Travis. I need you. But all of this is about you. Your anxiety. Your need to feel like God can fix this. And you've completely missed me."

Travis's style of relating is an example of spiritual bypassing, a form of spiritual abuse in which real emotions and deep pain are avoided in favor of a spiritual panacea. In place of doing the hard work of lament and grief, this person prays or fasts or prescribes a spiritual remedy, always on the lookout for the fix. As the most pain avoidant of all nine faces, he is quick to distance himself from his own pain, let alone the pain of others. The person struggling will feel disconnected and may even feel abandoned in her moment of grief.

This face of narcissism is grandiose in its optimistic sense of what might be, entitled in its sense of God's promise to answer prayer, and unempathetic in its posture toward pain, whether the individual's own pain or the pain of others. One of the great pioneers of the Enneagram system, psychologist Claudio Naranjo, viewed this as the narcissistic type within its unique personality system.[18] This person skips across the surface of life, continually bounding toward the next experience, incapable of honoring the present moment. While his energy may look like that of the winner (Type Three), his drive is not toward an achievement but an experience.

And while he may be the life of the party, those closest to him often grow weary. In church systems, he may be the pastor who constantly envisions a new ministry and mission, twenty steps ahead of those who need time to process and to consider the implications. In some cases, he may consider himself specially enlightened, the wise guru who sees the future when others only see the challenges. He may be irresponsible, ignoring details or abusing finances or engaging in addictive behaviors. He may be impulsive, charting new courses frequently. This type is most prone to addictive behaviors or experiences that foster a sense of transcendence or limitlessness. Food, drink, and sex are typical addictive pathways.

Ultimately, those who come into contact with this person may feel a baffling mix of self-doubt ("Why can't I think, lead, imagine, accomplish things like he can?"), confusion ("He does some good things, but I'm also hurt by him"), and exhaustion ("I can't keep up with his lifestyle"). Often, in order to change, it takes pain in his life so great that he can longer avoid it.

GUT TYPES (ANGER)

Type Eight: The challenger. The challenger is more often than not a leader, a person who likes to be in control, assertive, and strong. His opinions are firm, his presence is large, and his power is palpable. Of course, this is not, by definition, narcissism. In a healthy form, it may make for bold leadership. But it can make a potent cocktail for narcissism too.

While healthy leaders may display both strength and humility, the narcissistic challenger is invulnerable and potentially shameless. He lives his life to avoid weakness, and that requires him to protect any vulnerable or fragile part of himself within. He displays classic traits of a grandiose, overtly narcissistic personality disorder in his sense of superiority, his preoccupation with power and status, his expectation of others' compliance, his arrogant behavior and attitudes, and his interpersonal exploitation.

The challenger struggles with curiosity and patience, thus meriting the name—one who is quick to challenge, to critique, to correct. Though experienced as insensitive, he is actually quite attuned to pain and injustice, and quick to respond. However, those who tend toward narcissism will respond reactively, not reflectively. One might look to the apostle Peter's quick action to protect Jesus, drawing his sword to cut of the ear of the high priest's servant.

Jim was an executive pastor whose success in the business world made him an attractive hire for Denise, serving in her first lead pastor role at a larger urban church. Having never managed a large staff, Denise looked to hire a "strong leader," as she put it, with the hope that whoever it was would take charge of an inefficient staff. However, within months some were complaining of Jim's bullying. Sandy, who directed the youth ministry, said, "I've never seen a worse bedside presence. He has no empathy, only opinions." Dick, a longtime pastor of discipleship, cited Jim's condescension in their meetings with one another, even though Jim was younger and had no ministry experience prior to this role.

When Denise sat down to discuss these issues with Jim, he allowed little time before he launched into a diatribe about her "weak, insecure leadership" and "fragile personality." Denise was devastated. When she brought this before her leadership council, they decided to look into it. Jim's confident, self-assured report renarrated his experience with Denise as the unfortunate result of her lack of leadership experience, contending that he was merely trying to help her grow. Feeling torn, the council sided with Jim, requiring Denise to hire a leadership coach and asking Jim to take even more responsibility. Denise resigned.

Those in relationship with the challenger often feel powerless to effect change. Because he can be forceful, convincing, and even exploitative, one may simply opt for self-protection rather than reconciliation, resignation rather than hope. The sad reality is that the challenger, at his core, longs to be loved at his greatest place of vulnerability. If he were open, he'd be comforted by the words of Henri Nouwen who writes, "We form a fellowship of the weak, transparent to Him who speaks to us in the lonely places of our existence and says: Do not be afraid, you are accepted."[19] Sadly, the challenger is also a protector, barricading his own fragile heart behind a powerful and impenetrable wall.

Type Nine: The wallflower. It may be a stretch for some to believe that this personality type may be prone to narcissism. Indeed, the traditional images of narcissism do not quite fit the often reserved, peacemaking demeanor of this person. Once again, we must lean into the more subtle and introverted aspects of vulnerable, covert narcissism.

This face of narcissism may be experienced as one who is distant, unempathetic, and passive-aggressive. Though outwardly displaying a calm demeanor, this person conceals an underbelly of anger, a simmering resentment that does not emerge as the challenger's power or the perfectionist's critique but as quiet judgmentalism. They secretly long for love and admiration, in the absence of which they may become self-pitying and judgmental. Cut off from their own emotions and primary needs, they can be relationally cold, alienating those closest to them. Under stress, they can become paranoid and anxious, inaccessible to loved ones and friends. Disconnected from their deepest selves, they avoid responsibility, projecting blame onto those closest to them. As the desert father Abba Poeman once said, "There is one sort of person who seems to be silent, but inwardly criticizes other people. Such a person is really talking all the time."[20]

Jana had always been seen as the nice one, the kind of person no one could ever have a problem with. She was a wallflower, consistent in her service to her church and family but socially reserved. Out of touch with her own needs, she often absorbed the drama of others, silently taking the punches of almost everyone in her orbit.

But there was a flipside to Jana. Some described it as a "quiet rage." Others said that she was the most cold-hearted person they'd ever met. It was noted that "she could make you pay" by simply being her silently angry self in your midst. And no one doubted that she was passive-aggressive, quick to tell others that she was fine, that she wasn't mad, or that it wasn't a big deal—when, in every instance, it clearly was.

What's ironic about this is that while the Enneagram Nine exhibits the least amount of overt power, she has a quietly covert and subtle power that can affect others. Those in her orbit may experience her judgment, her rage, her disappointment. They may feel confused, never knowing quite how she is feeling but getting a very direct vibe from her demeanor. Some will feel like they are walking on eggshells, while others will sense that she is making them pay simply by remaining cold and obstinate. Effective at cutting off her own feelings, she may deny others love, empathy, and intimacy. This subtle, manipulative power is far more potent than it appears.

In the church context, this type of narcissism can stifle communication, connection, and creativity as staff or worship teams or other groups feel the anger that is not being communicated overtly. Without words, this person has the power to force others to quit, resign, or comply. However, because her typical demeanor is pleasant, she can play the victim, pointing the finger at others with the firm belief that she'd never quite have the power to inflict the damage they contend she has inflicted. For this reason, this face of narcissism may be the hardest to read.

Type One: The perfectionist. "He always has to be right," she says, peering at him cautiously, expecting he'll fire back in an instant. But he doesn't, in part because I'm in the room and he's trying to cooperate. Yet he's seething. She can feel it. I can feel it.

With a condescending tone he says, "Now sweetheart, let's not be like that." His face is angled, his eyebrows furrowed, and he looks like a parent scolding a child.

"This is the game he plays," she says. "I'm married to a lawyer who can't have an honest, intimate conversation. I'm always on trial. But he is judge and jury."

He looks at me hoping that I, a fellow "logical male" (as he says later), will see through her "neediness" and "silliness" and help her come to her senses. When I don't reciprocate his "we're in this together" look, he shuffles uneasily. I sense that he won't feel safe with me unless I conspire with him, but his wife won't feel safe if I do. We're at a fragile moment, and it's difficult to know whether we're in a courtroom or a counseling room.

This story provides a small glimpse into an experience with a narcissistic perfectionist. Often smart, logical, and principled, the perfectionist's hunger for truth and goodness can bring order, stir others to a righteous cause, and even inspire. This type has the capacity to see that things are not the way they are supposed to be, and he can cast a vision for a better world. And yet the perfectionistic energy can turn toward judgment of the other, a knife wielded in service of righteousness but with toxic consequences. At his most narcissistic, he is cruel and condescending, self-righteous and moralizing, indignant and abrasively rageful.

It's important to keep in mind that the lawyerly and perfectionist false self is a protective mechanism for his feelings of not being good enough. Perhaps he was criticized for not being a "good boy." Perhaps she heard "bad girl" time and again. Underneath, there is a palpable sense of anxiety—*maybe I'm wrong, maybe I'm deficient*. As we've said before, devastating shame lies beneath.

For those of us with traits of perfectionism but aren't diagnosably narcissistic, we might respond to a spouse's description with a repentant, "I'm so sorry I do that. I know that hurts you.

Sometimes I get so anxious that I feel like I have to control everything." But this becomes toxic when our personality becomes hijacked by the compensatory false self of perfectionism. The narcissistic Enneagram One will do anything to protect himself from being or feeling wrong, from feeling the sense of shame-based deficiency that underlies the strategy of being perfect, good, and right. Susan Krauss Whitbourne writes, "Not only can you expect your narcissistic friends, lovers, and family members to want you to be perfect, but you can anticipate that they'll externalize their own feelings of weakness by laying them onto you. If your partner is concerned that he or she looks tired, stressed, or messy, these concerns will translate into criticisms of how unkempt and fatigued you look."[21]

This profile of narcissism may show up more frequently in the church. The command-and-control profile of this narcissism mask reminds me of megachurch pastors I've consulted with, as well as corporate CEOs, founders, politicians, and lawyers. I've also seen it in the guise of the hardworking, blue-collar guy who works ten-hour days and expects a big meal, a few beers, and sex from his dutiful spouse when he gets home. I encountered it years ago in a fortysomething woman whose reputation for perfection propelled her restaurant to the top of the charts but alienated chefs and other employees. I've seen it in a rage-filled coach as well as a missionary mom who made her kids line up like the von Trapp kids in the *Sound of Music*. Further, it can become a collective characteristic of particular religious communities. Indeed, Steven Sandage and Shane Moe note that "some particular spiritual communities might perpetuate cycles of narcissism and shame by promoting spiritual perfectionism and validating shame-based scrupulosity and self-punishment."[22]

CONCLUSION

Understanding how the Enneagram intersects with the narcissistic personality stretches our imagination beyond caricatures. We're invited to see the unique manifestations of narcissism in personalities not typically witnessed as grandiose or attention-seeking. Indeed, you might have seen someone you know in the descriptions above.

Years ago, I was working with a woman who kept defending her husband, a seemingly soft-spoken rural pastor, even as I named aspects of his relating and behaving that were hurtful and even harmful to her. For years, she felt belittled and disrespected by him, often terrified but unsure why. He'd come and go unannounced. He'd drink too much and mutter a mocking comment to her under his breath. He'd poke fun at her weight, and he'd withhold financial resources from her. Years of being emotionally battered dulled her desire for more.

He was a quiet man with immense power. His bruising blow did not come in the form of a grandiose display but through a well-targeted whisper. His parishioners revered his quiet authority. She was crushed under it. Eventually, she quit counseling. Her husband had convinced her that her need for it was an obvious lack of trust in God.

If I had the categories I have today, I might have noticed the dynamics of a fearful and submissive Type Six bending to the will of a quietly angry and abusive Type Nine. That's a hunch, at least. But what I'm crystal clear on is that she experienced narcissism's vicious bite.

The faces of narcissism are more diverse than we typically imagine. And as we'll see in this next chapter, when they show up in one who is believed to be called to lead God's flock, people and whole systems experience the devastating impact.

FURTHER RESOURCES

Beatrice Chestnut. *The Nine Types of Leadership: Mastering the Art of People in the 21st Century Workplace.* Brentwood, TN: Post Hill Press, 2017.

Christopher L. Heuertz. *The Sacred Enneagram: Finding Your Unique Path to Spiritual Growth.* Grand Rapids: Zondervan, 2017.

Helen Palmer. *The Enneagram in Love and Work: Understanding Your Intimate and Business Relationships.* New York: HarperCollins, 1995.

CHAPTER FOUR

CHARACTERISTICS OF THE NARCISSISTIC PASTOR

*It is a terrible thing when such a one gets the idea
he is a prophet or a messenger of God or a man with a
mission to reform the world. . . . He is capable of destroying
religion and making the name of God odious to men.*

THOMAS MERTON

S tephen pastors a twenty-five-hundred-member church in the suburbs of a major city. During his ten-year tenure, staff have encountered his vacillations of charm and rage, fierce retribution amidst perceived disloyalty, a dictatorial leadership style, and personal habits of alcohol abuse and demeaning sexualization. Former staff and leaders started a private Facebook group to vent their stories of frustration and abuse. Most felt he would never be held accountable for his actions. However, mustering courage, several current and former staff members banded together to bring formal accusations against Stephen.

His immediate response was to own, in a general sort of way, his "mistakes over the years," but he did this while subtly casting doubts on the credibility of his accusers. Soon enough, the story went public on social media, and fans of his books and sermons came to his defense, acknowledging his humility and imploring people to live "by grace" in the way Stephen had taught. Meanwhile, the elder board became anxious when faced with the prospect of losing Stephen. Reports of sexual misconduct were covered up. Other influential pastors and Christian personalities came to his defense, eventually disheartening those who'd brought the charges. Stephen remains the pastor today.

A story like this provokes rage and a sense of injustice. Some who read it might say, "He's talking about my pastor." Others may see familiar characteristics in recent scandals that have rocked evangelical churches. All of us ought to agree that this is not the kind of person who should be shepherding God's flock. And yet in my experience this story is all too common, a testament to the fact that we've still not dealt with the pervasive reality of narcissism among clergy.

As Diane Langberg notes, the mantra of a narcissistic spiritual leader is, "I am bigger, I am better, and I have no interest in understanding my impact on you except in so far as you can feed my ego."[1] Of course, the grandiosity of a narcissistic pastor only hides his long, dark shadow. The church planters I've interviewed, for instance, often experience a strong "call from God," affirmation from others, and obvious gifts to communicate, inspire, attract, and influence. However, the narcissistic pastor's shadow side holds shame, rage, self-doubt, inner chaos, and intense fear—the fear of not being enough, the fear of not living up to their own expectations or the expectations of others, the fear of moral or vocational failure, the fear of not being right. The shadow never goes away; it's always lurking beneath, a constant reminder of a fragility the pastor would rather not admit. In the end, the threat of humiliation and shame keeps the narcissist self-defended and in control.

Of course, shame is the massive iceberg that exists below the water's surface. Because the narcissist is often incapable of real intimacy, opportunities for false intimacy and self-soothing are pursued. Addiction is often a form of control, a way of validating the narcissist's omnipotence.[2] I've consulted for many churches where influential, charismatic, and popular lead pastors who preach grace struggle privately with addictions, including extramarital affairs, substances, gaming, eating disorders, gambling, pornography, exercise, and more.[3] Even more, the narcissist's sense of self-identity may be his greatest addiction. Lasch writes, "The narcissist cannot identify with someone else without seeing the other as an extension of himself, without obliterating the other's identity."[4]

The narcissistic shepherd of the flock is a danger to it. The prophet says as much in Ezekiel 34:1-4:

> The word of the Lord came to me: Mortal, prophesy against the shepherds of Israel: prophesy, and say to them—to the shepherds: Thus says the Lord God: Ah, you shepherds of Israel who have been feeding yourselves! Should not shepherds feed the sheep? You eat the fat, you clothe yourselves with the wool, you slaughter the fatlings; but you do not feed the sheep. You have not strengthened the weak, you have not healed the sick, you have not bound up the injured, you have not brought back the strayed, you have not sought the lost, but with force and harshness you have ruled them.

Instead of taking care of the flock, the narcissistic pastor tends only to himself. He profits from the flock, failing to offer self-sacrificial love. He shows no care or empathy. Indeed, this passage reminds us that clergy narcissism is not a new phenomenon.

Narcissistic leaders display a constellation of troubling characteristics. Throughout this chapter, we'll look at commonly identified features of narcissistic pastoral leadership. While not exhaustive, they paint an accurate picture. And while a narcissistic pastor may not check every box on the list, I see the large majority of the characteristics we'll explore in leaders with narcissistic personality disorder (NPD). In their helpful book *How to Treat a Staff Infection: Resolving Problems in your Church or Ministry*, Craig and Carolyn Williford identify six primary characteristics:

1. All decision-making centers on them
2. Impatience or a lack of ability to listen to others
3. Delegating without giving proper authority or with too many limits
4. Feelings of entitlement
5. Feeling threatened or intimidated by other talented staff
6. Needing to be the best and brightest in the room[5]

While their list is quite helpful, I've identified four additional characteristics we'll explore as well:

1. Inconsistency and impulsiveness
2. Praising and withdrawing
3. Intimidation of others
4. Fauxnerability

Let's look at each of these in greater detail.

ALL DECISION-MAKING CENTERS ON THEM

Eugene Peterson tells the story of requesting a year-long sabbatical.[6] Not only did he get it, but the church was fine without him. He disconnected and rested. They continued to worship and serve. Peterson didn't check in every few days to make sure the budget wasn't cut or to vet the substitute preachers or to find out whether people were attending. He stepped away. Indeed, he was secure enough to step away, able to empower his people to lead in his absence.

A narcissistic pastor cannot step away. In fact, in his mind he is essential in every decision. While he may speak of a vision that empowers the laity and staff, his actions say otherwise. Unlike the apostle Paul, who trained and commissioned others to travel, preach, and shepherd on his behalf, the narcissistic pastor cannot relinquish control. His hidden insecurity manifests in anxious, hypervigilant leadership in which significant meetings or decisions cannot happen without his blessing or presence. Often he arranges leadership structures and polity in such a way as to protect his authority at every level of decision-making.

When a large suburban church initiated a ten-million-dollar building project, the senior pastor, Chet, designated his executive pastor, Randy, as a manager of the project. But as I soon learned while coaching Randy, he was no more than an errand boy or, perhaps, the eyes and ears of the pastor so that he could maintain control. This came to a breaking point when Chet unleashed on his executive in a fit of rage after a decision had been made about carpet in the new sanctuary. Though Randy had a team of qualified designers and gifted lay advisors who made the decision, Chet demanded a change, discouraging those tasked with design. An older lay leader who idolized Chet said, "We've got to trust his decisions. After all, he follows the Lord so closely." Indeed, the pastor's supposed spiritual authority is often cited or invoked to defend his right to decide.

IMPATIENCE OR A LACK OF ABILITY TO LISTEN TO OTHERS

Narcissistic pastors are often impatient with process and thus impatient with people. With a sense that "it should have happened yesterday," his leadership can be harsh and brutal, as the prophet described it, particularly with those he is called to shepherd. If a staff team is not quick to get on board with a new idea, or if a staff member doesn't get back to him right away after a text message is sent, he can be quick to the draw. In the end, his impatience reveals an absence of empathy. In his self-referential reality, others are a mere commodity.

Further, because he ignores his own limitations, he is impatient with the limitations of others. Because people are being used to prop up his authority and power (thus hiding his own limitations), their failure to respond promptly or affirmatively is a threat to his sense of competence and control. The narcissistic pastor sees others as an extension of his own ego and is unable to respond with curiosity, empathy, or compassion, in part because he has none for himself.

With this, however, the narcissistic pastor will renarrate his own impatience as decisiveness, and rebuff accusations of a lack of empathy with his own accusations about "weak" or "selfish" staff members who aren't good "team players." Unable to accept responsibility, he always has a take on the other that demeans and dehumanizes. Staff members who depart will almost always be subject to the narcissistic pastor's slanted narrative that privileges his special perspective.

When on a Friday afternoon a lead pastor tasked a few team members with the job of designing compelling visual displays of the new budget for Sunday's congregational meeting, they responded simultaneously with looks of dejection and exasperation. The pastor, unempathetic as usual, lectured them about the "mission" and reminded them that he had to preach, do two baptisms, and lead the meeting on Sunday. They relented. But then a series of life circumstances prevented two of the three from engaging the project. Left alone, the sole display designer fell into a panic and texted the pastor with her regrets—the visuals would not be done in time. Surprisingly, he seemed understanding. And yet on Sunday when he went up to present the new budget, he smiled and stated in a passive-aggressive tone, "Unfortunately, Jan, Melanie, and Jeff were responsible for designing the visuals, but they didn't get the job done." Winking at them, he added, "Perhaps we know where the budget cuts are coming this year." His public dig left the team anxious, confused, and ashamed.

DELEGATING WITHOUT GIVING PROPER AUTHORITY OR WITH TOO MANY LIMITS

When Jill was hired on to her first "real" pastoral role, as she called it, she was thrilled. She'd previously been in nonordained roles in complementarian church contexts, but now in an egalitarian setting she felt unleashed to use her full range of gifts with a new sense of authority. Reggie, the senior pastor and a strong advocate for women in ministry, hired her with big promises but with a job description that lacked specificity. He narrated this as "freedom to live out your call unhindered." But as she'd soon discover, she was indeed hindered.

Within a month she felt overwhelmed by the sheer number of things on her plate. She started to feel like a glorified secretary. A staff colleague even started calling her "Reverend Secretary," a cynical comment born out of his own negative experiences with Reggie, yet nonetheless condescending and demeaning to his new colleague. When Jill asked for opportunities to preach, lead, or train, Reggie would always say, "That's coming." But inevitably, she'd be tasked with hosting a class he would teach, where she'd make a Costco run to buy snacks and arrive early to set up the room. When she finally called Reggie out on her ambiguous role, he said, "That's what I hired you for. Are you going to get all weepy on me?"

Many narcissistic pastors have little ability to empower others in meaningful ways. They keep staff in ambiguous roles, perhaps changing titles often or realigning structures. This is confusing and demoralizing for hardworking staff members. Most narcissistic organizations are fiercely hierarchical, and staff are seen as clear subordinates. In the end, the narcissistic pastor may see empowerment as a threat to his control and authority. He may be perfectionistic and unable to trust another to fulfill a task up to his standards. He may tease authority without actually giving it. Out of exhaustion and exasperation, disempowered and demoralized staff learn over time to stop asking.

FEELINGS OF ENTITLEMENT

Power, privilege, and entitlement are expressed in toxic ways by narcissistic pastors. This can be especially dangerous when the narcissist has the spiritual power of an ecclesial office. Indeed, he may be less questioned than a CEO or politician because of a spiritual sense of entitlement as a one "working for the Lord" (Colossians 3:23 NIV). The ecclesial authority prompts followers to a holy deference to his calling and role.

A young pastor moved to a large, center-city neighborhood to plant a church. He was the star at the assessment center, and alongside his beautiful wife was often called the future "face" of his denomination. The assessment process didn't pick up on his narcissism, even though his wife reported that he felt entitled to sex daily and that he felt like God owed him success in the city after laboring in his first call in a "far less glamorous" associate role. In fact, the church planting committee ignored major red flags because this young man had been all but consecrated by a big name, successful spiritual father of the denomination.

In his first months living in the city, he raised $250,000, promptly setting a budget with a category for "general church plant expenses." Out of this large general category, he took $25,000 to add to a home down payment, used $2,200 on a new wardrobe for himself, spent nearly $1,000 to rent an expensive convertible for five days to drive to a church planters conference, stocked his home bar for "hospitality," and put money down on an expensive dental procedure to straighten and whiten his teeth. Even still, the primary coach assigned to oversee the plant locally bought his lie that the veteran denominational leader didn't see a problem with these things.

I've seen far-ranging manifestations of entitlement. I've seen lead pastors with large offices with leather couches and custom-made furniture. Some feel entitled to special financial provisions—home down payments, unlimited expense accounts, exorbitant paid vacation time, and in some well-publicized cases, second and third homes, planes, even yachts. One pastor leased a separate apartment for his frequent extramarital hook-ups. They feel that normal limitations don't apply—overdrinking and overeating and justifying addictions to pornography or paid sex. As one pastor told me after being caught in an affair, "I felt that because I gave so much to God, I didn't have the boundaries or limitations he required for others." Another said, "Deep inside I dealt with so much shame and inner constriction that my outward addictions gave me at least some sense of being limitless."

Entitled pastors snap when pricked, however. Even the smallest pinprick of challenge or concern from another leads to defensiveness and self-protective strategies. Because the things he feels entitled to become extensions of his ego, the threat of external loss is felt in a deeply internal way.

FEELING THREATENED OR INTIMIDATED
BY OTHER TALENTED STAFF

Narcissistic leaders are notoriously insecure. While they project confidence outwardly, they mask a fear that it could all come crashing down, that they might be exposed as incapable or unsuccessful, that they'd be revealed as deficient. While exhibiting the typically grandiose and omnipotent traits, narcissistic leaders are often hypervigilant. Unable to trust anyone, they feign connection in order to woo followers. Yet they are always on the watch for disloyalty, and when they find it, they punish it severely. They may use their power to threaten others by warning that they'll be blacklisted, that they'll lose their livelihood, that they'll lose influence within the system, or that secrets known to the leader will be revealed. As Langberg says, "It's a burdensome charade—they cannot feed the sheep, they feed off the sheep."[7]

One narcissistic pastor often used the phrase: "Know your place on the org chart." While he'd woo staff members to his side by trusting them with his secrets, sharing confidential information, or treating them to lavish food and drink, any sign of disloyalty or any inkling of advancement that could undermine his authority or image would lead to a fierce and direct encounter. One of his young, talented youth pastors received a standing ovation after his first public sermon, promptly leading the narcissistic pastor to remove him from the preaching schedule for the rest of the year. Two years later the staff member was fired. The youth pastor was so traumatized that he left ministry altogether and now works as a barista.

NEEDING TO BE THE BEST AND
BRIGHTEST IN THE ROOM

Unlike other professions where narcissism is prevalent, narcissistic pastors walk the fine line of omnipotence and feigned humility. He wants you to see that he is the best and brightest, but he wants you to think he is a humble servant of the Lord. He speaks of justice, of faithfulness, of humility, but he longs to be the center of attention, where his need to be special is affirmed. This does not necessarily mean that he has the most education (or the best). The narcissistic pastor doesn't need the best education because he's self-educated, surrounded by books (some his own, prominently displayed), and proud to remind you of his unique vision, the brilliant constellation of church plants, the genius plan that he has implemented. When he speaks of his unique contributions, there is a hint of condescension toward other churches that, in his high estimation, "lack vision" or "don't have the talent we have." Of course, he is speaking of his talent.

His need to be special and grandiose is affirmed by his "talented" staff, who stay if they live in service of his ego and leave, often messily, if they do not. I recall a young staff member who was excited to be hired by a "hero" of his, a popular church planter who took him in, affirmed his abilities, allowed him to do research for his sermons and books, and eventually gave him a multisite to lead. But the young pastor made a dreaded mistake: he suggested, albeit modestly and hesitantly, that his site might better thrive on its own, disconnected from the multisite hub. The pastor snapped, "You were a nobody before I hired you!" The young pastor was promptly removed from the leader's circle and isolated from the lead pastor.

The narcissistic pastor is the only one who can occupy the limelight. Even if he publicly affirms someone, it's in service of his exceptional gift to hire talent or his brilliant vision for the church.

INCONSISTENCY AND IMPULSIVENESS

Inconsistency and impulsiveness could be two separate categories, but I've almost always seen them operate together in narcissistic systems and among narcissistic pastors. While narcissistic pastors love visibly successful projects and programs, they're often better at imagining and starting new projects rather than sustaining them. In a large multisite church, the lead pastor would claim he'd been given a vision for the church year just weeks before the expected launch, triggering a frenzy among administrators, site pastors, the communications team, and other support staff who were expected to execute it without flinching. At the same time, they'd juggle their other projects, also inspired and commissioned by the lead pastor, resulting in long hours and exhaustion. Amidst all of this, there was a never-ending anticipatory anxiety felt throughout the whole team that one person described to me as "that inevitable sense that you'll get an email or a surprise staff meeting announcing his next big thing right when you thought you were finally making progress on his last big thing."

For staff, this can feel like working amid a hurricane. The dizzying array of ideas and visions may be explained away by the pastor as "creativity" or "passion," but a pastor who doesn't see the impact of her hurricane winds on a staff will quickly find a tired, overwhelmed team. Indeed, some may be terminated for not keeping up.

One reason for this phenomenon is that the narcissistic pastor must live in a constant state of ego inflation. The long, hard work of building one thing comes with many disappointments, and thus is inherently ego deflating. Proposing and starting multiple things allows the narcissistic pastor to receive all the praise for the successes and blame "incompetent staff" for any failures.

Jen pastored an urban church committed to justice and engaged in activism. Her fierce commitment to justice gained attention, and she was a perpetual presence on social media promoting her work. While she was adored by those outside the church, staff and laypeople within the church struggled to keep up with her frequent vacillations. She'd shift from one high priority cause to another on a dime. When she did, she inevitably had a narrative about the previous cause she'd abandoned—that its leadership was incompetent or that they didn't "get it." Staff who felt confused or exasperated were shamed for not being courageous or committed enough. Staff turnover was blamed on immaturity, and because she was seen by many as specially prophetic and courageous, Jen wasn't held accountable for her frenetic leadership.

PRAISING AND WITHDRAWING

Amid the hurricane, those within the narcissistic debris field will experience a confusing vacillation between praise and withdrawal. The loyal soldier who hunkers down and does the bidding of the narcissistic pastor is sure to get praise. She is an extension of his ego, so the praise is mostly self-centered. Nevertheless, for an insecure staff member who wonders about her place in the system, the praise can feel reassuring. Moreover, there is a kind of reciprocal nature to this kind of narcissistic relationship that is mutually reinforcing. A subordinate's vulnerable narcissism, which is mired in shame and insecurity, can be reinforced by the grandiose narcissism of the lead pastor.[8]

Jill was a committed leader of a community group at her large suburban church. She was drawn to the church because of lead pastor Jim's "confident articulation of the gospel." Later she came to realize that her own story of abuse made her the perfect candidate to be lured into Jim's cycle of praise and withdrawal. Her poor marriage, coupled with her low self-esteem, led her to seek out Jim's approval and praise. With it, she worked harder and harder to lead well and to volunteer, eventually receiving an invitation to join the staff. By now she felt as if she had a special relationship with Jim, even a privileged one that other core staff didn't experience.

Thus, when she risked pushing back on an idea Jim had at a staff meeting, she did not anticipate the consequences. Over the next days and weeks, Jim did not address her, look at her, or return her emails or voicemails. Anxious about their relationship and sensing she'd done something wrong, she reengaged her old pattern and stroked his ego at a staff meeting. Jim was resilient, returning the praise to Jill and reengaging her. Only years later in therapy did she discover the mutually reinforcing narcissistic relationship.

INTIMIDATION OF OTHERS

Some narcissistic pastors are bullying intimidators who use their power to wield control. Over fifteen years of church planting, Trey recruited competent and capable staff members out of other churches who were enamored, at least from a distance, with Trey's powerful presence and innovative ministry in a cool city center. But they'd quickly learn that only one person in the system had a say—Trey. The loyal ones, mostly out of fear, became fierce guard dogs for Trey, which gave them some cover from his harsh and critical bullying. They'd laugh at his jokes, which often came at the expense of other less-loyal staff or supposed ministry competitors. Trey's unmitigated confidence left staff confused about right and wrong at times, prompting one staff member to say, "For a while, I thought he was so righteous, even inspired by God, because I'd never seen a human embody such certainty about matters of God." In time, many capable staff departed, some leaving ministry altogether, often traumatized and in need of clinical counseling to make sense of their experiences.

In the many churches I've consulted with, it seems that intimidation tactics share common characteristics across denominations, networks, theological positions, and more. Some intimidation tactics are more forceful and direct. Others are passive-aggressive and indirect. No matter the delivery method, those on the receiving end feel worn down and disheartened by repeated and consistent intimidation. Some will comply. Others may fight back. But too often the narcissistic pastor wins.

The narcissistic pastor can intimidate in direct ways with condescension, threats of termination, long stare downs in a staff meeting, cutting comments about someone's work ethic or appearance, or removing someone from a key position or visible leadership role. Bullying intimidators ordinarily lead in contexts with little ecclesial accountability, where they wield almost exclusive authority. I've most often seen bullies in nondenominational contexts, and many are the founders, planters, and entrepreneurs who guard their churches and organizations like the extensions of the narcissistic ego they are. They may make brazen comments like, "I can do anything I want" or "I'd still have a job tomorrow if they found out I was having an affair." They parade their power before (ordinarily) submissive staff and parishioners, who feed off of the egotistic confidence of the leader.

In more structured and accountable settings, a more subtle, yet toxic, form of intimidation is required. Indirect intimidation often occurs through isolation. If you cross this kind of leader, you'll find yourself on the outside, wondering about your future. He might not do anything you can tangibly point to, like a demotion or role change, but he will make sure you feel his disappointment. Sometimes intimidation happens through triangulation. Ignoring you, the leader will draw in your peers, ingratiating them through approval and attention, all the while planting seeds of distrust about you. Too often these leaders are able to create competition or comparison within the system that pits some against others, or which selectively and inappropriately shares critiques of some within the system to others. These can be maddening forms of gaslighting that exasperate the victim of intimidation, leading often to reactive forms of self-sabotage, which give the leader reason for demotion or termination.

FAUXNERABILITY

Twenty-five years ago, when I was just getting started, vulnerability was not a high value. Things have changed. But with a higher value on transparency, authenticity, and vulnerability in the church, there is a dark "flipside" that we need to be aware of, a phenomenon I call "fauxnerability." And this may be the newest revelation of narcissism's pastoral bite.[9]

Recently I listened to the final sermon of a pastor whose affair was found out the week after this sermon, and who committed suicide not long after. Strewn throughout the sermon were statements like "We're all broken and need the gospel" and "I'm a mess like you," along with talk about the power of God to transform our wounds like God had done for this pastor. Imagine the shock and sense of betrayal when the congregation found out about his year-long sexual relationship with a female admirer he had met while speaking at a conference. The discovery was followed by days of throwing his wife under the bus for "emotionally abandoning" him. In the end, his shattered narcissistic false self led him to the tragic conclusion that if that self was gone, he was gone. And so, he acted on this belief, ending his life violently. The self-hatred was apparent in his final act.

Fauxnerability is a twisted form of vulnerability. It has the appearance of transparency but serves only to conceal one's deepest struggles. A husband may talk generally about his sinfulness, but a significant addiction to pornography may be ignored. A pastor may share vague references to his battle with lust but be covering up an emotional or sexual affair. In one scenario I was involved in, an influential pastor whose wife left him fell on the sword, sharing with his congregation that his many "besetting sins" contributed to the marital pain. He began sharing their story with any listening ear, talking about his brokenness and sin in a seemingly repentant way, grooming his listeners into empathy and trust. When he got them in his grip, he took seemingly innocent but calculated swipes at his wife—for her impatience with him, for her raging anger, for her unforgiveness. In time, people came to see him as the victim.

Those who are fauxnerable, as it were, may appear psychologically sophisticated. They may know their type on the Enneagram, MBTI, Strengthsfinder, or DISC. Some even go to therapy, often to therapists who collude, simply polishing up their narcissistic false self. This can make it tricky to discern the difference between vulnerability and fauxnerability. Here are some distinctions to be aware of:

- *Contradictions.* Fauxnerable people are not consistent in their character.

- *Disclosures that focus on the past.* "I struggled with porn" or "I was such a mess." This isn't vulnerability. Vulnerability is about showing up courageously in the *present moment* with how you are currently affecting someone or experiencing your inner life.

- *Staged fauxnerability.* A fauxnerable pastor or leader may conjure up tears at will on stage but show little empathy or care face to face.

- *Victim mentality.* The fauxnerable pastor may blame his staff, a bad system, or a needy spouse.

- *Lack of curiosity.* Vulnerable people are curious. Fauxnerable people are defensive and reactive.

- *Oversharing.* An emotional dump is not necessarily an act of vulnerability but may in fact be a way of using you to engender sympathy or to take their side.

- *Self-referencing.* His fauxnerability is in service of his ego, not an expression of mutuality or connection.

WHAT NEXT?

Too often narcissistic pastors are rewarded for their charisma. Congregants do not always have categories for what they may perceive from the outside to be occasional inconsistencies, frustrating drama, troubling rumors, or arrogant behaviors. They'll forgive these things for powerful sermons, persistent success, and perceived authority. They will often defer to the narcissist's spiritual persona rather than her true character. And because narcissistic leaders appear so confident and certain, they tend to be believed. This is especially true of celebrity pastors, whose success in followers and books and influence is interpreted as blessing from God. Accusers can be seen (and narrated) as whiny, vindictive, and jealous.

There are often no clear ecclesial pathways for confronting narcissism. As in each of the cases in this chapter, it's not uncommon not only to miss that a pastor is diagnosably narcissistic but even to reward him. For those hurt by a narcissistic pastor, the pathways to justice may be few. Many victims need to remain silent to keep a job or to get a job in the future. Some are driven out of ministry. Sadly, systems of accountability may be complicit or naive.

The ten descriptors in this chapter only begin the conversation. While these general characteristics put words to patterns many of us who study pastoral narcissism see, narcissism comes in many faces, and its bite is unique for each victim. Many who read these descriptions will attest to their reality, but simple identification of an experience does not amount to healing. You'd be right to ask: But what do I do? What next?

My own experiences of narcissistic abuse have left me feeling small, powerless, terrified, crazy, exasperated, enraged, and ashamed. If you've experienced it, you've experienced trauma. Do not chalk this up to a "bad experience." Name it as a trauma that affects every single aspect of your existence. This is not an admission of weakness but an honest confession. In your weakness and vulnerability is an opportunity for healing.

Being wounded by a narcissistic pastor is a particularly painful trauma. Clergy hold a uniquely powerful role in our lives, and an experience of abuse (in whatever form) from a pastor or priest or ecclesial authority is a profound violation. Some will avoid acknowledging this trauma for months or years out of deference to a spiritual authority, second-guessing their own experience all the while. Others may acknowledge it but stew with rage and avoid the work of healing.

We began this chapter with a word from the prophet Ezekiel, who reminds us that shepherds can be harsh and brutal. While it is especially confusing to discover this about a trusted priest, a beloved rabbi, a respected local pastor, or an influential celebrity pastor, it is crucial that those who've been affected take the violation seriously, attending to the trauma. For the reader whose experience of this chapter is an awakening to a lived reality, it is time to engage your story with a therapist who is mature and skilled in trauma work. For those who see this playing out in active ways within the life of a church right now, the best course of action is to begin by addressing your own health in a safe therapeutic relationship where, with wisdom and care, you can reflect on how best to engage the patterns you are seeing in your pastor and church.

FURTHER RESOURCES

Steve Cuss. *Managing Leadership Anxiety: Yours and Theirs.* Nashville: Thomas Nelson, 2019.

Chuck DeGroat. *Toughest People to Love: How to Understand, Lead, and Love the Difficult People in Your Life—Including Yourself.* Grand Rapids: Eerdmans, 2014.

Stanley Grenz and Roy Bell. *Betrayal of Trust: Confronting and Preventing Clergy Sexual Misconduct.* Grand Rapids: Baker, 1995.

CHAPTER FIVE

THE INNER LIFE OF A NARCISSISTIC PASTOR

*Too often, the wounded boy grows up to become
a wounding man, inflicting upon those closest to him the
very distress he refuses to acknowledge within himself.*

TERRENCE REAL

A lmost every parent experiences that lovely moment when a child says, "Mommy, Daddy, my shadow is following me." I remember my daughter Maggie, maybe two or three years old, dancing around our driveway in the bright Florida sunshine watching her shadow dancing alongside her.

But the shadow dance is not just the stuff of childhood. Almost everyone (and every church or organization) that seeks to grow up faces that terrifying moment when we realize that our shadow never leaves us. We can ignore it, deny it, or repress it, but only for so long. To grow up, we must not turn from it but to it, to learn from it, grieve through it, and even claim its many treasures. As the poet Rilke writes so eloquently, "Perhaps all the dragons in our lives are princesses who are only waiting to see us act, just once, with beauty and courage. Perhaps everything that frightens us is, in its deepest essence, something helpless that wants our love."[1]

In psychological terms, the idea of the shadow began with the great Carl Jung (1875–1961), whose "depth" psychology awakens us to inner portals that we refuse to see. Our hidden shame, our secret motivations, our quiet rage, our burdening fears, our fierce passions—much of this is kept neatly tucked away, and that's how we like it. In my book *Toughest People to Love*, I introduce Robert Bly's concept of the long, invisible bag we drag behind us, that container for all we refuse to accept about ourselves. I said that the task of growth involves opening the invisible bag—which can be both frightening and full of wonder.

I first opened my long, invisible bag more than twenty years ago. Each week I'd sit with my therapist and explore the contents of that bag. I could because he was safe. Somehow, he created what psychologists call a "holding environment" in which my deepest shame, fear, anger, and more might find their way into the light. It is an experience that we take for granted: safety allows our resistances to relax, our hearts to become tender, our vulnerability to find a home.

Narcissists do not feel like the world is safe. They might not say it out loud, but this is their inner experience. While we all use self-protective strategies, the shadow dance of a narcissist is a dance of radical avoidance of anything that threatens his grandiosity, his control, his certainty. And while the narcissist lives self-defensively, threatened by any who might be a rival or postured to stay in the one-up position in every relationship, he is really most threatened by what is hidden within. At his core, he is a scared little boy. And yet he appears angry and controlling when the repression of the shame and rage within unwittingly reveals itself, turned on others and a world he is threatened by.

Terrence Real writes, "Too often, the wounded boy grows up to become a wounding man, inflicting upon those closest to him the very distress he refuses to acknowledge within himself."[2] When I work with narcissistic women and men, I find myself deeply curious. How was he wounded? Who hurt her? What messages did he receive in his earliest years? What is her inner narrative about herself?

And more often than not, I see a shadow that looms large. I see a long, invisible bag that stretches miles behind him. I see deep pain, as wide and as vast as the expanse between rage and shame.

SHAME AND RAGE IN THE NARCISSISTIC PASTOR

Time and again, I experience narcissistic pastors swing from shame to rage and back again, a predictable pattern of exposure and defense, of vulnerability and self-protection. And sadly, while the shadow side holds untold pain, it is often ignored, manifesting in high levels of defensive and angry self-protection.

To be sure, there are times when I'll experience a moment of tenderness from a narcissistic pastor. In our work, he may open the curtain ever so slightly to reveal a wound. In a rare moment of vulnerability, he may acknowledge how scared and overwhelmed he is. While at times I experience a rare moment like this as inauthentic or, even worse, manufactured, I do sometimes experience a very real glimpse into the illusive shadow.

Tanner was a tall, broad-shouldered man with thick, dark hair and a firm jaw. His short-sleeve patterned shirt was tight, his muscular arms begging to reveal an array of colorful tattoos. I'd seen him on website photos and videos, but in person I was convinced he'd been chiseled by Michelangelo and dropped into the twenty-first century. We sat together for three long hours, Tanner volleying everything back to me, playing the long game, unwilling to surrender. That is, until we stumbled on a vulnerability. Tanner softened immediately when I asked about his little sister, killed at the tender age of five when she, Tanner, and their middle brother were playing in the family pool. Tears welled up too quickly for Tanner to wipe them away. He whispered the words, "I could've done more. It wasn't enough." His fists clenched, rubbing his thighs.

This was that glimpse I longed for. I pressed in slowly, hoping he might see how universal this very old self-criticism was in his story. But I've been doing this work long enough to know that this glimpse is, more often than not, fleeting. For many, the smallest exposure activates the brain's amygdala. An inner alert warns him of imposing danger, unleashing the full resources of his intrapsychic defense system: *Red alert. Red alert. Danger incoming. Armor up. Be on guard.* The chemical cavalry is marshalled. Adrenaline, norepinephrine, and cortisol are released, marching to their positions to unleash energy, increase awareness, and provide the resources to endure a brutal fight.

I see it before me. His soft eyes turn vigilant. His jaw tightens. His shoulders broaden as he sits upright, on the defense. His words become direct, stern, certain. Though seemingly controlled, you can sense a torrent raging within.

Shame gives way to rage.

All it took in Tanner's case was a question I asked, a question that felt threatening, "Tanner, do you think that message that 'I could've done more, it wasn't enough' is still alive in you today?" Of course, I knew it was. I wanted to see if Tanner could connect the dots, if he was ready to learn from his story. But he wasn't. His words leapt at me, "Don't go using my sister's death to psychoanalyze me, Chuck. That's off limits." In shutting me down, he shut down any possibility of an honest inner conversation. After this exchange, I lost him. He wasn't even up for the volley. Arms crossed, he opened Twitter with a swipe of his thumb on his phone conveying the clear message that he was done.

Unless we become conscious of our unconscious, the ignored shadow and all it contains rules our lives, stifles freedom, and emerges destructively in our relationships with others.[3] It may contain unprocessed grief, self-blame, and profound shame, as it did with Tanner. It may hold trauma—an episode of abuse, the emotional scars of repeated beatings from a parent, the neglect of a mother. While the narcissist seeks control, he is secretly controlled by a shadow force he cannot conquer. His self-contempt may show up as quiet, brooding anger or visceral rage, but it will show up, hurting those he professes to care about.

Of course, while I'm trained to notice the shadow dynamics at work in the narcissistic pastor, those in the line of fire know little if anything about it. All they witness is the control, the anger, the bullying, the rage. In my qualitative research over the years, I've gathered dozens of stories heard over two decades of ministry. I'm particularly struck by the theme of shame and rage among high-profile, evangelical celebrity pastors—mostly men who've written books and have prominent platforms, who write blogs and record podcasts, all the while enslaved to an ignored shadow. Some of these men have experienced well-publicized falls from grace, but others are still quite active and adored. Often people will say to me, "I never knew *he* was capable of that."

Current and former staff members under narcissistic pastors write me quite often with their stories. Often, before the narcissistic pastor is exposed publicly, there are years of painful smaller encounters that are covered up. The stories I hear reveal the fear of those who've experienced the hidden and sometimes not-so-hidden rage of the narcissistic pastor. For example,

- "I was brought into a room of male elders, and the lead pastor undressed me emotionally. He told me that I was insubordinate and that if I wanted to keep my job I'd need to take a pay cut and agree to get counseling for my anger issues. My anger issues?"

- "I'm reaching out because I was recently fired. Your writing on narcissism makes me wonder if my senior pastor was narcissistic. I'm scared because I've been told if I say anything about him or the situation I'll lose my small severance. He's a bully. I don't know what recourse I have."

- "My pastor has a stellar reputation. Everyone follows him on social media and thinks he's so well-balanced on issues. But if I'm honest with you, he's unpredictable, passive-aggressive, and incapable of having a real relationship. His public persona isn't who he is in our office."

- "I know she's a celebrity now, and everyone thinks she's the most amazing pastor and writer ever. But it's all ego, Chuck. If we don't support her 'rise' in every way, we're somehow undermining her, and she's made it clear that we should find another job somewhere else."

- "My husband has told me that he will divorce me and publicly humiliate me if I ever say anything negative about him. I'm afraid that everyone loves him so much that I would lose everything if I ever told people what an abusive bully he is. I'm even scared he'll hurt me."

These are only five of the hundreds I hold. And what I hear, more often than not, is not a mild fear of these pastors, but terror. Staff members, spouses, elders, and even friends feel terrorized at some level. These narcissistic pastors hold power in a way that intimidates and silences.

It's striking and scary that the rage-and-shame dynamic is a prominent one that I and others are seeing among popular and trusted celebrity pastors. And it prompts the question, why is this so? And why do we follow them, flock to their churches, and even protect them?

My conviction is that the very energy that so vigilantly guards and represses the shadow is the energy with which they project their larger-than-life, charismatic, driven persona onto the world. Their energetic and dominant personas can be compelling, charming, and convincing to the masses. They often have the capacity to do and accomplish many things and can appear almost super-human to those around them. Their persona may even be interpreted as spiritual giftedness, a personality well-suited to plant an effective church or lead a large ministry or church.

Their self-assurance and energy may be contagious, drawing in followers and staff who idolize them. Those of us who do not feel as confident or self-assured may even be drawn to their confidence—the "ideal hungry" follower who lives vicariously off of the confidence of the powerful leader. Thus many followers are unwittingly set up for disappointment, betrayal, or abandonment when the omnipotent leader is revealed to be less than ideal.

Because so much energy is given to repressing the shame, guilt, sadness, sexual confusion, or other shadow contents within, this pastor is often the most impenetrable of all. He simply has too much to lose. To admit an occasional battle with lust or to acknowledge losing his temper is risky; to open the invisible bag in order to face his own terror is unbearable. Invulnerable, they live not by the humble strength of Jesus but by power and personality, an egocentric false self, constructed to dominate and never be dominated.

Tragically, some of these pastors leave massive and painful debris fields in their wake. Their victims are staff members and spouses, members of their small group, and friends who dare to speak truth. I know capable and gifted women and men who are no longer in ministry because of their abusive and harmful experiences with pastors like these. I know churches that were shut down, and members and attenders who no longer go to the church because of broken trust.

At the same time, I've known healthy large church pastors, even celebrity pastors, who empower rather than disempower, who are vulnerable, and who lead from their true selves, not their manufactured personas. It's possible. But given my experience, I remain cautious whenever I hear about venerated "star" pastors. I can understand why the apostle James cautioned the gifted by saying, "Not many of you should become teachers" (James 3:1).

SHAME, RAGE, AND THE PASTOR WHO ASSAULTS

As I sat with one of those so-called "celebrity" pastors during a season in which his church was evaluating his emotional health, he said something striking. "Why do you give a damn about me when there are plenty of pastors out there assaulting and preying on boys?" He wasn't happy being under the microscope, feeling as if his peccadillos didn't quite add up to the major transgressions of others. I said to him, "And yet, you assault with words."

There isn't a significant difference psychically between the pastor who assaults with words (or even with silence) and the pastor who assaults physically. The same dynamic of shame and rage is at play. Even in the case of sexual assault, the fundamental dynamic is one of power. Whether a pastor bullies with intimidating leadership tactics or manipulates through sexual grooming and assault, abuse is abuse.

When Sam, the well-regarded pastor of a fundamentalist Baptist church, was accused of sexually assaulting women he saw for pastoral care, the community was outraged—at the women who made the accusations. Sam was a fine orator, a "faithful preacher of the gospel" according to his parishioners, and a married man with four sons. How could *Sam* do something like this?

As it turns out, Sam was adept at slowly grooming his victims with compliments and flirtations. He made the women he saw for counseling feel like they were his highest priority. He cast suspicion on their husbands, imploring them to trust no one but him. He'd sexually assaulted eleven women in five years.

Why does a Catholic priest assault a young boy? Why does a youth pastor groom a high schooler in the youth group? Why does the "grandfatherly" elder of the church molest a child?

We often say that the perpetrator was living a double life. I often call it the "quadruple life," however. There is the *public self* we present to the world, the *private self* we share selectively with others, the *blind self* that is clear to others but which reminds hidden to us, and the *undiscovered self* which, like the shadow, contains unseen and unconscious aspects of ourselves.[4] Those who've explored their inner lives and family-of-origin stories are often the most self-aware, living congruent lives of integrity and wholeheartedness. But those who lack curiosity about themselves and remain largely out of touch with their feelings, needs, and unconscious motivations are most likely to project their hidden rage outwardly onto another.

Sometimes, when I write or blog on narcissists and abusers, I get responses that go something like this: "Why don't you just focus on how perpetrators harm? I feel like by talking about their shadow sides and inner pain, you're trying to convince survivors to have empathy for them or even let them off the hook." Let me emphasize that if you've experienced assault, I'm not trying to convince you to feel sorry for, forgive, or empathize with your abuser. If you ever do get to the point of empathy or even forgiveness, that will take a long time, a lot of therapeutic care, and plenty of honest lament and grief of your own in the process. What I am interested in, however, is helping all of us understand the psychological dynamics at play. It helps me to know a bit of what's at play within a narcissist when I'm dealing with one.

For example, I counseled a man named Richie, who engaged in an honest and difficult process of painful self-revelation. His narcissism emerged out of his own painful childhood, in which he was abused at truck stop men's showers while accompanying his father on road trips. This occurred between the ages of six and twelve. He began looking at child pornography in middle school, and by the time he was twenty-five he was grooming young, middle-school boys in his large, megachurch youth group. By forty, he was sitting in my office, having served fifteen years in prison.

Prison humbled Richie, though he hadn't been able to do the work of therapy he desired. Because he'd been so utterly humiliated through his trial and imprisonment, he was less defensive than almost any narcissist I've ever seen for counseling, and more ready to engage his own story of abuse. I was astounded, because though he hadn't done formal therapy while in prison, he clearly used his wide-open windows of silence for inner work. At one point, I said, "You've become a contemplative." He said, "I think I have." He'd been reading Thomas Merton and he clearly identified with Merton's language of the false self. He was curious about what lay underneath.

Richie's rage and shame story was about a little boy, utterly powerless, desperately afraid, and deeply ashamed. Afraid to tell his father (who was asleep in the truck's cab during these shower episodes), he unconsciously shut away his pain and became tough and emotionless. When he became a Christian in high school, the tears flowed: he felt loved and forgiven, and he thought he was healed. But he wasn't. A salvation prayer doesn't magically heal our shadow side. Richie realized that he continued to be drawn to boys even after he started working part-time as a church youth minister. He couldn't tell anyone. His shame was too great. At the same time, his rage was directed inward. "You're a terrible, awful, sick man," he'd tell himself.

On the outside, he was a charismatic and crafty manipulator who led worship passionately, drawing in adoring young admirers, feeding his ego with the attention and affection of his youth. On the inside, he was a frightened little boy, scared of his own shadow.

Abusers shame and humiliate; they do violence to their victims. In truth, they are creating on the outside what exists beneath their consciousness on the inside. Some avoid their shadow by cutting themselves, others by abusing substances, and still others by spiritually bypassing. But those who assault bury their shame so deep that their hidden rage turns outward. The harm they do traumatizes their victims and churches and destroys trust. By seeing what's happening on the inside, my hope is that we can move from reactive to preventative strategies for healing wounded women and men. I hope we are better equipped to "keep watch."

KEEP WATCH

As a seminary professor, I get to train pastors. I also get to participate in many ordination services. In my tradition, when a woman or man is ordained, they are "charged," implored to keep watch over themselves and the flock. Often a veteran pastor will read Acts 20:28: "Keep watch over yourselves and over all the flock, of which the Holy Spirit has made you overseers, to shepherd the church of God that he obtained with the blood of his own Son." The apostle Paul offered these words to a group of leaders, but I do think they're words for all of us, the priesthood of all believers. Each of us is called to grow up out of infancy and immaturity, as Paul says elsewhere, working in a unified way, building one another up, and identifying and tackling the obstacles to growth along the way (see Ephesians 4:1-16).

The phrase "keep watch" is sometimes translated "take heed" or "pay attention." This is quite different than "be paranoid" or "suspect everyone." We're not charged with perpetual suspicion but with attentiveness and awareness. The ancient imagery of shepherding is helpful—a shepherd wouldn't stay up all night watching every little movement of his sheep, but he would know his sheep so well that he could detect patterns, inconsistencies, or erratic behavior. Are we aware enough of ourselves and one another to do the same?

I've heard from churches who've said, "We never expected our lead pastor would do that" or "I can't imagine that she'd be capable of harming someone." Often I suspect that along the way people choose not to see things that might be troubling, especially in their leaders. Over the years, I've noticed that people choose to believe the best, overlooking possible inconsistencies, minimizing minor relational violations along the way, dismissing their own suspicions. For some, pastoral leaders are seen as spiritual authorities, holy and set apart, sanctioned by God, and thus above suspicion.

Saint Paul says, "Keep watch."

First, keep watch over yourselves. No real transformation can happen in your congregation without your own personal transformation. Sometimes your own inner work can open you up to psychological dynamics at play around you. Several years ago I worked with an associate pastor, a young man who presented with symptoms of depression. The depression masked feelings of profound inadequacy, often expressed through a narrative he'd heard from his senior pastor. After four years of working with his senior pastor, this young associate was now considering leaving the ministry, believing himself to be "untalented" and "too anxious" and "not winsome enough as a communicator." I challenged him to do the hard work of growing up. We identified all sorts of shadow baggage from his own life, and after a year's worth of therapeutic work he emerged much more self-aware and self-differentiated, more resilient, and quite clear about the abuse he was experiencing from his boss.

You don't need a degree in counseling to notice problem patterns and inconsistencies. You don't need a degree in organizational psychology to notice anxious systems and abusive dynamics. Each of us is gifted with an intuitive sense of right and wrong, health and unhealth. As God's image bearers, we're hardwired to recognize the scent of shalom and to wince at the smell of accusation and evil. While it's true that our own baggage can get in the way of our God-given sensibilities, this is all the more reason to do what's necessary for our own growth, much as the associate pastor did for himself.[5]

Second, keep watch over the *whole* flock. Pay attention to the whole—to the system, the community, the congregation. Attend to its health. Healthy churches simply do not hire narcissistic pastors. They can spot one a mile away. Healthy churches care well for their pastors, providing them with opportunities for regular rest and sabbatical, for continued growth opportunities, for retreats, for therapeutic care. And healthy pastors, in turn, care well for their sheep. They empower them, equip them, comfort them, feed them. They lead their churches in vital mission, caring for the vulnerable, engaging in the work of justice and mercy. While anxious churches driven by narcissistic pastors may grow numerically, healthy churches flourish. Do not mistake numerical growth for flourishing.

Third, be attentive to the little ones. I often recommend an organization called GRACE (Godly Response to Abuse in the

Christian Environment) for church education and training, particularly for the sake of our children (see netgrace.org). It is vital that churches stand vigilant for children, especially in the wake of recent public scandals, but also because there are frequent but lesser known cases across the United States and beyond in Catholic churches, evangelical churches, mainline churches, synagogues, and more. GRACE is also a good resource for churches wrestling with accusations against pastors, as they provide independent investigations and organizational assessments. Further, other organizations, like RAINN (Rape, Abuse, and Incest National Network), provide resources for sexual assault and trauma (see rainn.org). Proactive church leaders will equip staff teams, leadership, and congregations for wise watchfulness. My hope is that in the coming decade, every church will be committed to awareness, ongoing training, and practices of emotional and spiritual maturation.

As a seminary professor and a psychological assessor of clergy, I find it vital that seminaries, pastoral education programs, and nondenominational network training centers take pastoral health and well-being seriously. At my own institution, we begin this shadow work in a student's first semester. Each student is assessed rigorously by outside psychologists, and each is given a thorough face-to-face review with growth and treatment suggestions. When counseling is needed, we make it available and affordable. Students are invited into vital inner conversations through a formation curriculum that utilizes nonviolent communication to help students identify feelings and needs and develop personal agency to make healthy requests for what they need. They are required to do family-of-origin work, a one-week retreat through the Enneagram, and various seminars on sexual abuse and wholeness, addiction, racism, and healthy spiritual practices. And most of that is before the mid-program face-to-face assessment with formation staff and two faculty members!

Each of us must do our shadow work, but it's not a solo endeavor. Indeed, churches and Christian organizations that make it a normal and accepted practice cultivate health on multiple levels. No one church does this perfectly, but there are thriving, missional, and healthy churches that cultivate practices for personal and systemic health.[6] It's important to keep watch, not from a place of paranoia but of awareness, recognizing also that there many good churches, pastors, and Christian organizations pursuing wholeness for the sake of mission.

When we have courage to look in the long, invisible bag, we may find scary parts of ourselves, but we also discover hidden treasure, deep passions, and holy longings we may have missed. We are image bearers of a good and loving God who pursues our wholeness even when we're not aware of it. Our active participation in this pursuit is vital for ourselves, for the church, and for the world.

FURTHER RESOURCES

Justin and Lindsey Holcomb. *Rid of My Disgrace: Hope and Healing for Victims of Sexual Assault.* Wheaton, IL: Crossway, 2011.

Kathryn Flynn. *The Sexual Abuse of Women by Members of the Clergy.* Jefferson, NC: McFarland, 2003.

GRACE. Article and video resources. www.netgrace.org/resources.

CHAPTER SIX

UNDERSTANDING NARCISSISTIC SYSTEMS

*Imagine little earthquakes everywhere that
change the shape of everything distorted by
narcissism—that change the shape of us.*

SHARON HERSH

After a brutal season of late-night meetings and lay-all-your-cards-on-the-table conversations, the elder board decided to ask for Ben's resignation. Years of heavy-handed narcissistic senior leadership of the church led to multiple firings of "incompetent" staff. In the end, his wife's decision to not "stand by her man" revealed a fatal crack in the armor. He wouldn't be able to save his leadership role and his marriage at the same time.

As the remaining staff and elders gathered to survey the debris field, Rosanne—the current executive pastor—spoke for the team saying, "Finally, we've been purged of narcissism."

But in reality, the entire system was infected with it, and they didn't know it.

SYSTEMIC INFECTION

Many years ago, a simple infection in a friend's toe led to sepsis. The small infection invaded his bloodstream, triggering inflammatory responses throughout his whole body—a systemic infection. I was shocked to receive a call from his daughter alerting me to the life-threatening situation. How could a small infection impact the whole body?

So it goes with churches. Removing a narcissistic staff member does not necessarily remove the narcissistic infection. More often than not, sepsis has set in. You can't see it, but it lurks among the in-between relational spaces, in anxious bodies, and in flawed structures. It shows up in our inability to be personally and organizationally honest, to recognize the strengths and weaknesses of a church system, a denomination, or a network of churches. It shows up in our unwillingness or inability to take intentional steps toward systemic healing.

Rosanne's response was naive. In fact, while the staff of eighteen breathed a sigh of relief that the senior pastor had resigned, they did not use this moment as a time of personal and systemic self-assessment. Instead, they maintained a pattern of reactive leadership, choosing a path of survival rather than active reflection, interrogation, and adaptation. The anxious system looked for leadership, and several rivals stepped up for a shot at the new lead role. A weary elder board lacked the tools and resources to see the larger picture and picked the best communicator in the mix, hoping that people wouldn't leave *en masse*. No one thought to hit pause for a season of reflection. No one saw the systemic infection—that is, not until the same old patterns emerged in new forms.

Systems are powerful. They hide invisible forces that work below the surface. I'm trained to see these things, and when I approach a system from the outside I can often diagnose the dynamics fairly well. But I've operated within systems that have slowly strangled me, only awakening to this dynamic after a personal crisis or after leaving. Ronald Heifetz writes, "To diagnose a system or yourself while in the midst of action requires the ability to achieve some distance from those on-the-ground events. We use the metaphor of 'getting on the balcony' above the 'dance floor' to depict what it means to gain the distanced perspective you need to see what is really happening."[1]

Let's be honest, though. "Getting on the balcony" can be difficult when you're living in an anxious, reactive, narcissistic system. When you're in the middle of it, it is often easier to get with a couple of colleagues and triangulate about the silly decisions of another staff member. Even more, the grip of a narcissistic system can trigger a feeling of powerlessness or futility.[2]

TWO DIFFERENT NARCISSISTIC SYSTEMS

Just as the narcissist requires external validation to confirm how special or great she is, so a narcissistic system requires external validation for how special and great it is. A large church or successful parachurch ministry revels in the affirmation it gets on social media or at conferences. A successful capital campaign prompts a collective sense of pride that God is blessing us (and *not* that church across the street). This phenomenon is sometimes called "collective narcissism."[3] But, as it turns out, systems can be arrogantly convinced of their greatness or, paradoxically, vulnerably narcissistic in a twisted form of self-deprecating self-righteousness.[4] Let's look at both types of systems.

Grandiose narcissistic systems. In the first instance, a narcissistic system—whether a church, a denomination, a network of churches, a parachurch ministry, or another—delights in itself. Disconnected from the reality of the system's dysfunction or narcissistic sepsis, the members collude in a collective act of glancing lovingly into the pool of water that reflects back the ideal image, just as a narcissistic pastor might.

How does this happen? In these systems, there are often seasons of supposed blessing, manifesting in growth or financial health or recognition of some kind. Sometimes these systems are led by narcissistic leaders, but this is not always the case. Some systems have a reputation or brand beyond a leader, a pastor, or a CEO.

For instance, a parachurch organization I consulted with had many strong leaders over the years. Each was chosen for his ability to perpetuate the ministry's reputation and grandeur. He or she became the "face" of the system. Each of the leaders lacked self-awareness—that is, until Matt took over. Matt was a distant friend of mine, but he reached out when he realized what he'd gotten himself in to. He admitted that he was enamored with the role and title he'd inherited as the next leader of the ministry but had little idea of the dysfunction he was witnessing before he took the job.

That dysfunction was in fact a collective and systemic form of grandiose narcissism. While the mission statement of the organization spoke of serving Jesus and the kingdom, the ministry existed to perpetuate its impressive, but complex, mix of discipling, resourcing, and equipping churches. The multimillion-dollar budget confirmed to everyone who worked there that they were leading the way, that God had granted success. Each person in the system fed off of the grandiose posture of the organization.

Matt's first whiff of narcissism came as he sensed a void, an emptiness in their work—a lack of "gospel vibrancy" as he named it to me at first. As he surveyed staff members about their personal sense of mission, he rarely heard anything related to a call to follow Jesus. Indeed, he was alarmed by a collective narrative that went something like this: "The [rival ministry] is doing that, so we must respond by doing this." He heard key leaders within the organization talk in disparaging ways of the other ministry, he read personal blogs of his staff that mocked other Christians while elevating their own work, and he felt what he described as a "gross arrogance" at staff meetings. He told me that staff-meeting culture felt more like game planning to beat the rival than corporately discerning God's will for that season of ministry. He said, "It seems as if they're all in some sort of group trance."

While a narcissistic leader can be removed from his or her role, a system is not easily dismantled. As I engaged this work, we first attempted to discern whether or not there was any capacity for self-reflection among the key staff. In a team meeting of seven key leaders I recall asking them to describe to me weaknesses of their organization. Their responses were surface level and shallow. Weaknesses included an accountant who could be replaced, a slow response time in delivering a needed resource to a denomination, and a former executive director who didn't have the "get up and go," which apparently cost the organization time and money. I asked them what made their organization different than a secular, for-profit business, and each told me that their "kingdom focus" was the difference. But there was no clear sense that this so-called kingdom focus looked anything like the upside-down, self-giving way of Christ. It looked more like a cut-throat corporation than a Christlike ministry.

Rigorous self-reflection is imperative for any system to change. The transformation of a system requires transformation among its members and, most importantly, transformation in its leader (and leadership).[5] In a sense, change can only occur from the inside out, as those invested in the change process experience transformation themselves. In Matt's ministry, there was a lack of spiritual and relational vitality that deprived them of the needed resources for self-reflection. Habituated to the narcissistic organizational patterns, each new staff member quickly became absorbed into its infectious forcefield. Some staff members I interviewed did not realize that spiritual vitality had been sucked from them until we engaged in an honest deep-dive into their personal story of experiential intimacy with God. Many were susceptible, having arrived there without a vital spiritual life and with the hope that working at a Christian ministry might help them. They all seemed to need the jolt of confidence they got by identifying as a member of this organization.

In working groups of four or five folks, we began to discern themes that we recognized as long-term, universal problems with the ministry. In a relatively short period of time, consensus was building that there was a problem, and that each person within the system was a part of it. Insight led to ownership, which led to a shared sense of investment in a new way of going forward. Even Matt surrendered any sense of certainty that he could or should lead the organization going forward. But Matt's commitment to personal transformation was infectious, and a collective sense of affirmation fueled a renewed sense of call for Matt. One of the most beautiful moments came when key staff leaders shared their own personal stories of grief and repentance, which organically led to a corporate time of prayer and repentance bathed in tears and confessions.

Grandiose systems often resist change, however. They resist because grandiosity works. Integrity gives way to pragmatism; honesty gives way to illusion. The status quo is much easier than the work of becoming self-aware, evaluating, naming reality, letting go, grieving losses, and embracing new pathways. Add to this the toxic groupthink that resists divergent voices or conflicting visions and you have a recipe for a resistant and perpetually septic system.

Vulnerable narcissistic systems. In the first instance of narcissistic systems, a collective arrogance marks the organization's culture. It needs to feel special, to be the best, to succeed. But there is another picture of narcissistic systems that may not be as familiar. Earlier in the book, I defined "vulnerable narcissism" as a narcissism that manifests in subtler, sometimes shy, ashamed, sensitive, passive-aggressive, and victim-based ways. Vulnerable narcissists secretly clamor for affirmation and adoration, but instead of claiming these as a matter of arrogant entitlement, they manipulate and maneuver in ways that are just as toxic and harmful. This instance of narcissism manifests in systems too and is sometimes called "low self-esteem narcissism."[6]

A vulnerable, low self-esteem narcissistic system, while not as transparently arrogant as its countertype, resists health by choosing to engage in masochistic and self-sabotaging patterns. In church systems, in particular, I've witnessed a kind of twisted theological justification for this. These systems will speak of humility, sin, dependence on God, and embracing weakness in ways that defy gospel definitions of them. What is labeled as humility looks like self-deprecation. What is defined as weakness manifests in woundedness. And dependence on God becomes an excuse for passivity and blame when things don't go well. In the end, the lack of health inevitably leads to pain for its leaders and its members.

A hundred-person church in a university town in the Midwest boasted of its commitment to "faithfulness to the inerrant word of God." But identity in the church and on staff seemed to center on a shared imagination of how bad they were. One elder said, "These other churches are so humanistic, but we know how sinful we are." While other churches were exploring pathways to vital mission, this church had a commitment to *not* doing whatever other churches were doing. Indeed, this church expected that they wouldn't grow or thrive like others and were instead rigorously committed to preserving the "truth" despite systemic dishonesty and unhealth.

For decades, the guilt-and-shame-based culture of the church attracted both pastors and parishioners who shared this pathological complex, buttressed by a theology that affirmed human badness. And to participate in this culture, one needed to be predisposed to opposition. So, when a young, fresh-out-of-seminary pastor was called whose theology and disposition aligned, the match was sealed.

Kevin looked and talked like a sixteenth-century Reformer. His hipster beard covered a twenty-five-year-old face which, as it turns out, was a face full of shame. For a year and a half, Kevin's firebrand sermons impressed the hard-to-impress hardliners and wooed a new generation of women and men who needed their inner criticism confirmed from the pulpit. The narcissistic masochism was strangely attractional in that town, and newcomers quickly confirmed that this was a church that took theological orthodoxy seriously. Though they cherished a belief that they were the only really honest church when it came to the seriousness of human sin, a supposed high-theology of individual sin masked the systemic sins of judgment, racism, misogyny, tribalism, passive-aggressive intimidation, arbitrary threats of discipline, and emotional and relational avoidance.

Theologically approved bullying was inflicted by headship-affirming husbands toward their "helpmate" wives, by certainty addicts against the theologically wishy-washy, and by moralists against anyone crossing their invisible fences. Kevin spoke disparagingly of his elders, the elders spoke disparagingly of the congregation, and the congregation spoke disparagingly of their neighbors. It was a tormenting cycle of negativity that came to a head when Kevin's depression and emotional affair with a former girlfriend he found through Facebook came to light.

Not surprisingly, the church responded to Kevin's situation with a narcissistic sense of "how could this happen to *us*, to the true church?" An already anxious system responded with typical reactivity—"He must not be one of us, after all." They imagined that, in order to fall like he did, Kevin must not have believed as strongly as they did. There was no curiosity, no compassion, and certainly no grace for Kevin, whose employment was terminated. He was quickly ushered into an ecclesial trial that was punitive and shaming. I met him two years later, as he and his wife were still licking their wounds, having not yet dealt with their pain in therapy because they were suspicious of psychology.

Kevin eventually took courageous steps to deal with his pain and brokenness but reported that the church called yet another young firebrand to fill his shoes. As Kevin awakened to his own chronic shame, his eyes opened to the sepsis in the narcissistic system he had worked within. "It was a setup," he said. "I wasn't the first. I won't be the last, it seems. But it was a perfect recipe for disease and disorder."

Vulnerable narcissistic systems, while not as blatantly arrogant, display a quiet self-righteousness that is just as troublesome as grandiose systems. In some ways, they can be more resistant to change than the grandiose system. The rigid belief systems and arrogant certainty of a vulnerable system often demand a high level of allegiance along with painful consequences for those who leave the system. However, in both systems the tug toward loyalty and uniformity is strong.

WHAT DOES A HEALTHY SYSTEM LOOK LIKE?

As we see the effect of grandiose and vulnerable narcissistic systems, we might be prone to discouragement. We may wonder what a healthy system or structure looks like. Are there practices or principles that characterize healthy ecclesial systems?

First, healthy systems—whether ecclesial systems, nonprofits, or secular organizations—value and build up everyone in the system, maximizing the benefits for all without exploitation. In narcissistic systems, success benefits some and not others. The weakest within a staff or congregational system are subject to exclusion, abuse, and more. But the apostle Paul imagines the church as an interdependent body. He imagines it growing in maturity, moving from infancy to full maturity, writing in Ephesians that the church's shepherds are called "to equip the saints for the work of ministry, for building up the body of Christ, until all of us come to the unity of the faith and of the knowledge of the Son of God, to maturity, to the measure of the full stature of Christ" (Ephesians 4:12-13). The evidence of ecclesial health is that *everyone* is built up, growing in maturity, moving from the emotional dysregulation of infancy to emotional and spiritual centeredness and stability in adulthood.

Second, while success in its healthiest sense is valued, it is not accompanied by grandiosity and exhibitionism. As we've seen, Christian institutions and churches are susceptible to the same grandiosity as secular organizations. Grandiosity is an illusion, based not in facts but in a delusion that works on a personal or collective level. The healthiest systems resist delusion and live in radical honesty, no matter the consequences. As two organizational researchers have written,

> The healthy narcissistic organization remains fact-oriented and tries to discover the "truth" of a situation by examining both supporting and disconfirming evidence. The healthy organization is open to the possibility that it enjoyed a success because of luck, or a failure because of its own mistakes. A healthy organization's identity will not be unduly threatened by a short-term failure because it possesses a healthy

confidence that it will succeed in the long term. Because it is reality-based, a healthy organization will be much more open to change than its dysfunctional counterparts.[7]

Missiologist and educator Ed Stetzer echoes this in a series he wrote for *Christianity Today* on surviving unhealthy Christianity. He paints a picture of a healthy family system: "I was struck by their health and sense of family. Even as they disagreed, the focus was family and graciousness in their disagreement. People were allowed to ask questions, leadership was transparent, and trust was present."[8] When a system is not dominated by anxiety, everyone is free to speak truthfully, everyone is free to listen curiously.

The ten-thousand-dollar question is always, "How do we achieve this?"

An addict who has been through recovery will tell you that the first step is the hardest. People and organizations who admit to a problem will often find that a huge weight is lifted, but they'll often resist this as long as possible. A large Presbyterian church in the South felt this burden, recognizing that they were mired in long-term toxic traditions and septic patterns that were hard to break with. It took a group of representative members at a congregational meeting—including an elder-father of the church, a coffee-elitist millennial, and a working mom—to have the courage to approach the mics and say what needed to be said: we're sick and we can't settle for band-aids anymore. Sometimes health begins with the prophetic act of truth-telling.

Systems willing to be brutally honest are systems ready for newfound health. In this church, the bold and courageous people who came to the mic were recognized as loving truth-tellers, motivated by the church's health and not by their self-serving agendas. The congregation's trust in them led to a collective agreement to enter into a transparent process toward health guided by an outside consultant. This church entered into a courageous process of becoming self-aware, evaluating, naming reality, letting go, grieving losses, and embracing new pathways.

Third, the leadership's health must be assessed. I'm often amazed when I'm invited to help a church or staff or system to find that the senior leader wasn't expecting to contribute anything other than his expert opinion of the problem. I remember asking one leader, "Are you willing to participate in the assessment as well?" His look of fear, rage, and puzzlement said it all. To his mind, I was not there to assess him but to solicit his omniscient perspective. Yet I've never seen systemic health emerge apart from the leader (or leaders) going on their own transformational journey. Might that journey include therapy, spiritual direction, coaching, or more? Perhaps. Indeed, the leader willing to lean into self-discovery is the leader who will inspire others to that work.

Fourth, a system inclined to health demonstrates a relentless curiosity, particularly in its solicitation of other perspectives. One of the finest examples of this I've ever seen was in a suburban context that featured two very large churches, quite a few middle-sized churches, and some smaller churches hanging on for dear life. Everyone had an opinion of the largest church in town. When a scandal was uncovered involving its popular and charismatic youth pastor, the community was abuzz. A newer senior leader of this large church seized this moment as an opportunity for radical honesty. He invited the pastors of almost every nearby church to a two-hour session in which he and a few of key internal leaders would listen to their experiences of this church. He introduced the time as an opportunity for each person to share the good, the bad, and the ugly—how each person there had experienced this church, its leaders, its ministries, and more.

Though reticent at first, the anxiety was broken when the solo pastor of a small church chimed in. He said, "I've fought seasons of anger, resignation, and shame around your church. We were a church of 150 ten years ago, but your programs drew people away. I've had to let really good staff go. I've wondered if any of you recognized your impact on all of us. I've also experienced seasons of immense gratitude. My next-door neighbor came to faith in your church. Your mercy program is transforming lives. But today is remarkable. That you would invite me here to share with you that I'm angry, and that we can together talk about how you become healthier is good for you, good for us, good for our entire community." The honesty continued as pastors brought specific examples of hard experiences related to the large church in crisis. The lead pastor and his team took notes, listened intently, and asked good questions.

In the end, they didn't have a statement to make. They didn't have a solution. Instead, the pastor expressed his deep sadness around the church's failures, his gratitude for stories of hope, and his intent to stay connected. And he did. Over the next year, he took many of those who spoke to lunch to hear more feedback. This slow but important process changed the complexion of the church, and resulted in massive shifts in partnership, collaboration, relationship, and trust in the church community.

A MOMENT OF RECKONING

As I write, the Catholic Church is embroiled in scandal. Investigations into clergy malpractice are revealing decades-long patterns of abuse and coverup among bishops, cardinals, and all the way up to the Vatican. As I write, the evangelical church is wrestling with confusion, disbelief, and anger surrounding Bill Hybels, Willow Creek Church, and a pattern of abuse and coverup that impacted many women over many years. Hybels was heralded as a leader among leaders and his was an organization that shaped leadership imagination.

Respected celebrity pastors are navigating scandals involving adultery, abuse, gaslighting, plagiarism, financial malpractice, and more. The collective false self is powerful, and it covers a mountain of hidden rage and shame. I do not know many of the people and players in these scenarios well enough to diagnose narcissism, but they prompt more than a little curiosity and wonder.

Might we be in a moment of reckoning? Twenty years ago, when I first encountered narcissism, it did not seem that the church took it seriously, and I wonder if we are ready to address it today. As a clinician, I see ecclesial narcissism at levels that alarm me.

I also see how ordinary lay Christians can be blind to dangerous and toxic narcissism in political leaders, whether on the left or right. There is a dangerous collusion with power, and I'm mindful that amid our own anxiety and shame, we unwittingly align with unhealthy and powerful leaders who offer us a false sense of control and identity. While I see pockets of the church taking narcissism seriously, I am not ready to say that we're collectively primed to look in the mirror and confess our corporate participation in narcissistic systems.

A friend and author, Sharon Hersh, writes eloquently about many things, but when she muses on narcissism she often uses the hashtag #ThisIsAboutUs. She refuses to see narcissism as a problem in *them,* but rather views it as an issue for *us* to face:

> We have learned to live in the grip of narcissism. We are proud and we hide. We want God and we want to be god. We bless and we wound. We fall down and we dare greatly.

We resolve to stay off Twitter because we're afraid of what it might reveal about us. We pose for selfies and know that we are posing because there's not enough of anything to make us truly enough. We need a tectonic shift to an interconnectedness that invades every nook and cranny of our lives. Can we raise children that aren't entitled? Can we talk about politics without dividing family and friends? Can we believe in God without leaving some people out? Imagine little earthquakes everywhere that change the shape of everything distorted by narcissism—that change the shape of us.[9]

Sharon is diagnosing not just individual narcissism but our collective narcissism. This is about us. Indeed, we all participate in narcissistic systems. Perhaps these systems are part and parcel of the "powers and principalities" (Ephesians 6:12 KJV) with which we contend. Perhaps they're all around us, not just in church systems but in our corporate and political institutions, even in our looser social media connections and broader tribal identifications. Perhaps this is about us, an invitation to wake up to the many ways in which certainty trumps curiosity, uniformity trumps unity, hubris trumps humility, control trumps connection, loyalty trumps love.

With Sharon, I pray for little earthquakes everywhere that shift us, break us, and transform us.

FURTHER RESOURCES

Jim Herrington, Mike Bonem, and James Furr. *Leading Congregational Change: A Practical Guide for the Transformational Journey.* New York: Jossey-Bass, 2000.

Terrence Real. *I Don't Want to Talk About It: Overcoming the Secret Legacy of Male Depression.* New York: Scribner, 1998.

Shelley Reciniello. *The Conscious Leader: Nine Principles and Practices to Create a Wide-Awake and Productive Workplace.* Greenwich, CT: LID, 2014.

Peter Scazzero. *The Emotionally Healthy Church: A Strategy for Discipleship That Actually Changes Lives.* Updated and expanded edition. Grand Rapids: Zondervan, 2010.

Miroslav Volf. *Exclusion and Embrace: A Theological Exploration of Identity, Otherness, and Reconciliation.* Revised and updated edition. Nashville: Abingdon, 2019.

CHAPTER SEVEN

THE GASLIGHT IS ON

Spiritual and Emotional Abuse

*Traumatized people chronically feel unsafe inside their
bodies: The past is alive in the form of gnawing interior
discomfort. . . . They learn to hide from their selves.*

BESSEL VAN DER KOLK

Gaslighting is a form of emotional abuse that draws its name from a 1938 British play called *Gas Light*. In the play, a man named Jack Manningham terrorizes his wife, Bella, by making her doubt her perception of reality. Bella is comforted only by the one reality she can trust—the dimming of the gas lights that correspond with Jack's afterhours antics. Among his antics, Jack hides household items and blames her for misplacing them, which throws her into perplexion and self-doubt. Her only shred of sanity is in the gaslight's flickering flame, and the audience is held in suspense as she vacillates between self-doubt and clarity.

Those affected by the bite of the narcissist do not feel it right away and may even think they deserve it. The narcissist develops the uncanny ability to make others feel crazy, uncertain, confused, insecure, and bewildered. Sadly, this occurs in a variety of contexts, not least in the church.

In this chapter I highlight the subtle, even spiritual, forms of emotional abuse perpetuated often by those on the narcissistic spectrum as we look at the key features of narcissistic abuse.

A STORY OF ABUSE

They looked as if they'd be cut out of an advertisement, a Ken-and-Barbie type of couple whose tan complexions, bright smiles, and flirty disposition made me wonder if I was being set up. I was a young therapist, engaged in my first set of church planter assessments, and I was just suspicious enough to think that the experienced assessment team might toss in a couple of actors to test the new kid.

Zak and Andrea been introduced to me as shoo-ins for the assessment. Zak had raised close to $150,000 in just a few months, and their church plant was primed for a launch in just a few weeks. I sensed that the testing I'd do was just a formality, that with a wink and a nod we'd push them right on through. After all, their sending church was one of the largest Presbyterian churches in the South, and it was a key supporter of the church planting center I was hired to consult for. I was anxious, not just because I was a rookie, but also because I smelled a foul odor.

Zak and Andrea took the standard assessments, followed by their one-on-one appointments with me. Zak came in first, tall and lean, filling up the room with charm and swagger. He was twenty-seven years old, a kid, but the darling of the church planting world. "So, what do I need to work on, Doc?" he said. I wasn't yet finished with my doctoral degree, and I sensed his move to ingratiate himself with me. He wanted to appear compliant. But I had some hard news to deliver—troubling elevations on his psychopathology assessment, along with disconcerting responses from Andrea, raised the real possibility that I would not be able to approve them.

I was anxious. If I delivered the hard news, I'd likely lose my good standing with the assessors and others who believed him to be a rising star. If I didn't, I'd forfeit my own integrity.

The next hour was brutal. I felt like I was at war. Zak began with a false sense of compliance, pretending to be curious, to listen, to acknowledge aspects of the findings. I said, "Zak, your elevations on the narcissistic spectrum are significant, and I . . ."

He interrupted, "Looks like I've got some work to do between raising money and raising leaders, Doc!"

He'd repeat this pattern of interruption, quick to explain or defend. He did not seem curious and showed no humility. I sensed that he saw our exercise as an obligatory one, and I sensed an entitlement that concerned me.

When we turned our attention to their marriage, he anticipated Andrea's response. "She was pretty tough on me, I suspect," he said, shaking his head in disgust and pity. "Can I be honest with you, Doc? I'm worried about her. She bucks my authority, and we know how that can be as guys, don't we?"

I was stunned by his presumption. My biggest concern now was for Andrea. She'd been playing a part, and now she'd privately waved the red flag, her desperate attempt to get the young assessor to notice. Zak's beautiful wife was no longer willing to be his Barbie doll, his puppet on a string, his teddy bear to be cuddled at one moment and tossed about the next.[1] She sat literally feet outside of the room, waiting for her verdict—either validation or dismissal. I felt the pressure.

Zak did too. He raised the money, received the endorsements, and was seen by many as the next big thing. He'd go to the center city, emulating the successful strategies of other city pastors, and start the church. I suspect that he saw much more in his future too—a book deal, speaking engagements, maybe the keynote for church planters in ten years. But his face was now red—a raging red that accompanied an intimating glare. I hadn't gone in to expose him, only to be curious, to draw him out, to see if the testing matched my experience of him. To my chagrin, it did. I was now walking on eggshells, anticipating his rage.

"Tell me as honestly as you can if there is anything at all troubling, from your perspective, about your treatment of your wife," I said. I expected nothing, but he volunteered some things.

"Doc, I can be harsh, but for her sake," he told me. "She's lazy. She needs to understand how vital our work is for the kingdom. It's her self-focus that hacks me off. She needs to be mission focused, eye on the ball. My anger is for her edification."

I paused, silently considering my final words. After a moment, I said, "Zak, this interview is by no means a deal breaker—I don't have that power—but it's a major speed bump. I need to meet with Andrea, and then we'll need some time together to consider next steps. But my testing and this interview gives me significant pause. I cannot recommend you at this time."

The room was silent. Thirty seconds. One minute. Zak's head was down. I said, "It's time, Zak. We'll talk more later."

He looked up, gazing as intensely as I've ever experienced another man's angry glare.

"Her word against mine. After all, there are no bruises," he said.

TRAUMATIC EMOTIONAL ABUSE

Perhaps the most frightening thing about narcissism's bite is that it often comes without leaving a physical wound. The trauma inflicted can look like humiliation, hypercriticism, silence, exclusion, affairs, flirtation, jealousy, extreme mood swings, crude jokes, constant jealousy, bargaining for love, guilt, shame, control of finances, sexual manipulation, blame shifting, isolating one from friends and family, threats, boundary violations, and much more.[2] This is by no means an exhaustive list, but it illustrates the complex reality of psychological/emotional abuse. While physical scars or bruises may not appear, psychotherapist Daniel Shaw writes that "what is always present is the invisible, interior pain inflicted on the other."[3]

When I share a list like this with a victim who is just coming to terms with the reality of traumatic narcissism, it can be overwhelming. A rush of emotion floods over them—repulsion, self-doubt, shock, confusion, terror. She may tell me that a movie played on fast-forward through her head, with key memories, including nauseating sexual encounters, threats, major boundary violations, or particularly ugly put-downs. Our bodies hold these memories, and when the trauma is triggered a flood of memories can rush into our conscious minds. Trauma expert Peter Levine writes, "Although humans rarely die from trauma, if we do not resolve it, our lives can be severely diminished by its effects. Some people have even described this situation as a 'living death.'"[4]

While I will suggest some resources at the end of the chapter that can help us further understand these experiences, it's important to explore how narcissism and traumatic abuse meet when they come to church. I don't think it's an overstatement to say that the place where traumatic, emotional abuse is most misunderstood, outside of the US court system, is in the church. For twenty years I have worked with dozens of women who've looked to the church for empathy and safety, only to find doubt and disbelief. I've worked with men trapped in abusive marriages or toxic work environments who are ashamed to name the reality, often because they believe men need to be tough and strong. After all, "there are no bruises."

While the trauma theorist Bessel van der Kolk argues that "emotional abuse . . . can be just as damaging as physical abuse and sexual molestation,"[5] women and men who experience this within churches can be portrayed as hypersensitive, prone to exaggeration, dishonest, delusional, and ultimately untrustworthy. Many will not ask pastors for help for fear of a negative response. In my many years of treating clients abused by narcissistic spouses, I can count on two hands the number of times churches stepped up with courage to offer empathy, care, safety, and resources.

Sadly, sometimes the church's response only reinforces the trauma. Levine writes, "Trauma is not what happens to us, but what we hold inside in the absence of an empathetic witness."[6] In therapy, we can invite the Spirit to be an empathetic witness, and I will often invite my clients to recognize that God is more near to them than they are to themselves, as St. Augustine said. The Spirit dwells with them and in them and among the many shattered pieces within, bearing witness to narcissism's bite, and holding them compassionately. But trauma victims struggle to know any kind of safe intimacy, let alone intimacy with God.

The scars of emotional abuse are invisible, but no less real. As I got to know Andrea, I quickly realized that Zak was not her first abuser. He was the most recent in a long line of emotional abusers dating back to her childhood. Andrea's father never touched her sexually or beat her physically, but he bombarded her with criticism. She was never good enough, pretty enough, active enough, spiritual enough, obedient enough. Her father, a recovering addict, fought his own battles with shame, remedying his own powerlessness by being a bully to his children.[7] In time, Andrea began looking to boys to meet her needs for affection and love. She found young men who gave her a taste of what she needed, but who sensed her low self-esteem and used and manipulated her. By now, she'd experienced the cuts of a thousand invisible knives. She numbed her pain in depression, overeating, and moralistic Christian books. It didn't help. I was the first person to name her abuse.

Andrea and others who experience this kind of devastating, ongoing abuse too often find their profound trauma minimized by well-meaning Christians. Comments like, "Well, at least you weren't sexually abused" or "God protected you from something worse" only serve to minimize and deny the real trauma that victims experience. Van der Kolk writes, "Traumatized people chronically feel unsafe inside their bodies: The past is alive in the form of gnawing interior discomfort. Their bodies are constantly bombarded by visceral warning signs, and, in an attempt to control these processes, they often become expert at ignoring their gut feelings and in numbing awareness of what is played out inside. They learn to hide from their selves."[8]

They learn to hide. It's the age-old story.

When pastors and churches deny the impact of emotional abuse, they retraumatize the victim. When we defer to suspicion of a victim and support of a potential abuser, we run the risk of doing irreparable harm. Victims may shut down or return to their abuser. They may blame themselves for being too much trouble.

Sometimes the wily narcissist is just spiritually nimble enough to convince the pastor that while there have been a few mistakes, it's all very reconcilable. Well-meaning pastors who want to be helpful may inadvertently fall into the powerful trap of a narcissistic abuser, buying their pleas for grace, intentions to do better, or fauxnerable expressions of regret. In the absence of clearly visible signs of abuse, the pastor might think the victim is exaggerating. Or, not understanding the traumatic impact of emotional abuse, he may prescribe band-aid solutions—praying together, reading a Christian book on marriage, date nights—all in an effort to help.

My continual prayer for the past twenty years has been that pastors, ministry leaders, and churches would resource themselves about the silent killer of traumatic emotional abuse. It is tragic that this kind of abuse finds such fuel in the church.

TRAUMATIC SPIRITUAL ABUSE

Years ago I was a given a copy of *The Subtle Power of Spiritual Abuse* by David Johnson and Jeff VanVonderen and, with a wink and a nod from a mentor, was told to go and read. First published in 1991, the book arrived on the scene during a time of political transition and rumors of war, increased international media attention of sex scandals in the Catholic Church, and American televangelist scandals. The world was feeling a bit less safe. The church was feeling a bit less safe.

Johnson, a pastor, and VanVonderen, a therapist, shined a bright light on the church's complicity in an insidious form of emotional abuse—spiritual abuse. Without casting doubt on the veracity of the gospel's ancient story, they dared to name spiritual manipulation and coercion, shaming tactics, control, and condemnation. The book was and still is a go-to for many in ministry, an illuminating and honest guide to a sinister shadow side of the faith. After reading it, my work with Christian clients and parishioners would never be the same, as I saw scars carved by those I'm supposed to call sisters and brothers in faith.

Spiritual and emotional abuse have much in common, but spiritual abuse bears a particularly sinister twist, as principles and maxims of faith are wielded as weapons of command and control, and faith leaders abuse their power for the sake of feeding their own unmet emotional needs. The victim feels just as perplexed and confused as one who has experienced emotional abuse but experiences it from a seemingly more authoritative source—a holy source.

I've seen particularly harsh examples. I've counseled a woman serially raped by her pastor-father while he recited prayers over her. I've seen a pastor-husband for therapy who punished his wife for not having sex with him by masturbating behind his church pulpit. I've held the stories of young men groomed and molested by priests and youth pastors. I've walked with a group of women as they reported a legendary missionary for years of sexual assault.

But most spiritual abuse happens in seemingly mundane situations. Often I work with someone who sees her Christian upbringing as pretty ordinary and normal until we begin exploring the effect of a belief system or the influence of a powerful spiritual authority. Because we tend to implicitly trust church or pastoral authority, we often do not question experiences that may in fact be shaming or anxiety producing, or even violating.

One of my former students discovered this as she did her Genogram for my class. The Genogram is a tool for exploring one's family of origin; it can be a powerful means to self-discovery. Through her Genogram interviews with family members, this student began to notice a distinct pattern of shame in all of the women in her extended family. She encountered themes of subordination to male spiritual authority, silence in the face of criticism, private battles with depression, and unexpressed resentment hidden beneath a veneer of spiritual cheerfulness. She named this "generational spiritual abuse," and committed to doing her own inner work to end the destructive generational pattern.

Spiritual abuse can include some or all of the following characteristics:

- *Silencing.* Spiritual authority is invoked to silence someone because of their gender, a difference of opinion, or a rigorous hierarchy. Those who speak may be scolded and will likely feel shame around having a voice or opinion.

- *Moralizing.* Legalism in service of abuse is particularly harmful, as strict codes of behavior or moral expectations are elevated above trusting relationship. The victim will internalize a sense of shame around who they are when they cross the artificial boundaries of a spiritual abuser.

- *Certainty.* A belief system is offered as inerrant and infallible, the only valid expression of the Scriptures, and a member's good standing requires signing off on the whole of the belief system. There is often a tribalism in which the church or denomination has the truth and others do not. If anyone deviates or raises questions, they are shamed or ostracized.

- *Experientialism.* The most spiritual people have the most ecstatic experiences, and those who don't are questioned, marginalized, and made to feel like they don't have enough faith or aren't as blessed by God. They are made to feel deficient and wonder why God wouldn't give them the same experiences.

- *Unquestioned hierarchy.* Hierarchy in abusive situations isn't empowering but disempowering. Those who are not in charge are made to feel small, insignificant, and unenlightened. Some may wonder why they're not good enough or smart enough to be given some authority or at least to be considered.

There are other characteristics of spiritual abuse, but these are fairly common. And, indeed, if you're committed to spiritual health and integrity, you'll be rightly angered that these are all-too-frequent experiences within the church.

Jesus was angered at the spiritually abusive tactics of the Pharisees. In Matthew 23, he expresses anger and lament through eight "woes." Jesus says that the Pharisees put loads on other people that they themselves are not willing to carry, that their lives are characterized by grandiosity and ego rather than humility, that they win people over to their faith only to further enslave them, and that they give their money to the church but neglect the more important matters—justice, mercy, faithfulness. Matthew 23 could have been written today. Times may change, but the tactics for abuse seem recycled from generation to generation.

YOU'RE NOT CRAZY

The common thread in each of these descriptions is a victim who feels ashamed, deficient, confused, self-doubting, and crazy. These experiences in a relationship are always a signal of some kind of toxic pattern—but untangling the web of relational toxicity is often a time-consuming and burdening affair. It requires a deep investment in seeking the truth, both in oneself and in the toxic relationship.

Not long ago a client told me that the most important moment in our three years of counseling was when I told her that she wasn't crazy. I've probably said this to dozens if not hundreds of victims. Yet she reinforced the importance of those words amid her unique story of gaslighting in her marriage.

Anyone who experiences a sense of shame or deficiency ought to exercise some curiosity about its role and origin in their story. In this broken world each of us will experience these emotions in some form, and they're not an immediate indicator of abuse. No parent is perfect. As my daughters begin their transition from high school to college, I'm mindful of all of the mistakes, missteps, and mixed messages my wife and I have sent them. As much as I believe that my daughters trust that my love for them is real and secure, they've certainly faced my neediness, fragility, anger, moodiness, and emotional absence. I've had to own these things time and again.

I do not want to use the language of abuse lightly or frivolously. When I consider the soul-crushing effects of gaslighting and emotional/spiritual abuse, I see *intent* and *impact* as important factors for discernment. A good parent will make mistakes—and then own those mistakes, through repentance and a real empathy and care for a child. A good pastor will make mistakes—and then own those mistakes, once again with sincere repentance, and with a real curiosity for how she's hurt others. However, abusers intend to stay in a powerful, one-up position. Their abuse is more than a momentary behavioral lapse; it's a pattern of violation or oppression or crazy-making. Their intent is revealed in a deep need to be in control, to remain invulnerable at the expense of the other.

And their intent is often seen in the impact they cause, especially over time. Abusive, crazy-making behavior confuses and confounds. It violates the freedom and dignity of another. It is intended to break the will of the other, and it often succeeds. And this is why we must take gaslighting with a deadly seriousness.

Let's conclude by returning to the story of Zak and Andrea. I received a phone call from the lead assessor not long after the assessment. He said that the committee had recommended Zak with an expectation that the supporting agency would help fund his church plant. He said to me, "We expect that you psychologists will be extreme—you're always looking for what's wrong versus what's right. God's up to big things with Zak. He's a bit rough around the edges, but I don't see anything that a good coach can't work out with him." Dejected, I hung up the phone and told my wife I'd prefer never to do another church planting assessment again.

Today Zak is divorced and no longer in ministry. His wife left him three years after the church started. She began to take his gaslighting and emotionally abusive tactics seriously, and after several attempts to get him into therapy, she called his bluff and told him she was leaving him. Zak spent the next weeks calling Andrea's faith and sanity into question. And then, a turning point.

Zak's children's ministry director and worship pastor both decided to step courageously into the melee. They'd experienced Zak's abusive patterns in their day-to-day ministry life. They too had felt as if they were the problem. But Andrea's bold decision led to painful and honest conversations with each other, with Andrea, and then finally with a governing body of their church. When Zak heard, he was incensed. He called into question the competency of the governing body, which led to an intervention from one of his original supporters. Thankfully, the structures of accountability around Zak worked this time, and he was asked to step away from ministry for a year to address his personal and marital issues.

Zak didn't just get moody on occasion or lose his temper once or twice a year. Zak abused. Zak gaslit. Zak manipulated. Zak refused accountability and scapegoated others. His victims felt the impact of his relational pattern; they felt narcissism's bite.

There are many who need to hear the words, "You're not crazy." And now is as good a time as ever for the church to begin taking the phenomenon of gaslighting seriously. Woe to us if we don't.

FURTHER RESOURCES

Diane Langberg. *Suffering and the Heart of God: How Trauma Destroys and Christ Restores.* Greensboro, NC: New Growth, 2015.

Lundy Bancroft. *Why Does He Do That?: Inside the Minds of Angry and Controlling Men.* New York: Berkley, 2002.

David Johnson and Jeff VanVonderen. *The Subtle Power of Spiritual Abuse: Recognizing and Escaping Spiritual Manipulation and False Spiritual Authority Within the Church.* Bloomington, MN: Bethany House, 1991.

Wade Mullen. Research and writing on the language of abuse, particularly in Christian organizations. https://medium.com/@wademullen.

CHAPTER EIGHT

HEALING OURSELVES, HEALING THE CHURCH

Blessed are the poor in spirit, for theirs is the kingdom of heaven.

JESUS

When Paul was fired from his first pastoral position after three years, his body felt stiff and frozen. Hired to be mentored by the lead pastor and eventually deployed as a church planter in the city he'd felt called to, he felt strung along over three years, disempowered and exasperated in his work under Bart, a narcissistic pastor. Was Bart threatened by him? He wasn't sure, but he heard whispers that the church plant would never happen. When he asked for a meeting to address his concerns, Bart agreed. But when he showed up, Bart was seated beside a lawyer, a senior elder in the church, who presented Paul with nondisclosure and noncompete agreements he'd need to sign on the spot to receive a short, three-month severance. Failure to sign would mean immediate termination, and a not-so-subtle threat by the lead pastor to tarnish Paul's reputation in the planting network that had originally affirmed his gifts. His hands shaking, Paul picked up the pen and signed. Bart smiled affirmatively, extended his hand and said, "Blessings brother. You'll land on your feet."

Stacy entered her third year at a conservative seminary, hopeful that it would be different. While a few men in her class supported her, many others were adamant about their views regarding female pastoral leadership. One of the professors seemed hellbent on making her experience intolerable. The system itself seemed to conspire against her success, but she pressed on, hoping to attain her Master of Divinity and pursue ordination. But it began again—anonymous notes left on her desk, hostile comments in class, a low grade on a paper she felt deserved an A, comments like "at least she's nice to look at." As the semester unfolded, she experienced growing depression, insomnia, and panic each day as she entered the seminary building.

Heather sat with her husband Len in their pastor's office, as they'd done dozens of times before. The walls of that office held the secrets of a marriage filled with terror—loud drunken outbursts by Len late at night after coming in from his shop in the garage, abusive comments about her appearance or cooking or parenting, then promising that he'd get his act together or recommitting to praying and reading his Bible regularly. Each time, Pastor Tom encouraged Heather to forgive and "do her part" to heal the marriage. This time Len ashamedly admitted that he had made out with a girl at the bar two nights prior, stumbling through a face-saving apology. Heather, clear and strong, said, "No more. I'm done, Len. You need to pack your bags tonight and stay with your brother while I figure this out." Quickly, Pastor Tom interjected, "Now, Heather, you're not going to kick out a repentant man. Maybe you need to assess your own unforgiving heart."

Paul's, Stacy's, and Heather's situations will be familiar to many who've been impacted by narcissists or narcissistic systems in the church. In each story, the toxic combination of low empathy and unhealthy power has inflicted pain and trauma that will last well beyond the encounter.[1] Those hurt by the narcissists' behavior will need care in ways they cannot realize at the time, as the symptoms of their trauma cascade for days, weeks, and even years beyond. In this chapter, we'll explore a vision of healing and wholeness amid the pain and trauma of narcissism. First, we'll look at a biblical and psychological pathway for healing. Then we'll revisit the stories above, looking at them through the lens of this pathway.

THE HEALING JOURNEY

For me, the narrative arc of the Exodus journey has become an immensely helpful paradigm for healing. I wrote about it in my first book, *Leaving Egypt: Finding God in the Wilderness Places*. As a mental model for change, the Exodus story allows us to see ourselves, and our congregations, as pilgrims on a healing journey. It invites us to see the enslavement that keeps us from thriving. It invites us to be brave enough to cry out to God. It invites us to the risky journey, fleeing what is familiar for an unpredictable path ahead. It invites us to have patience in the face of a long and winding wilderness road. It invites us to lament in the face of continued pain. It invites us to resolve to enter a new land, a hope-filled place of flourishing. Indeed, all stories of transformation necessarily take us on a cruciform (cross-shaped) journey, imitating the life, death, and resurrection of Jesus, as we become participants in his suffering in order to experience his resurrection (Philippians 3:10).

Each of us, first, must take whatever "Egypt" we're living in seriously. As we've seen, living in the grip of a narcissist can be immobilizing. We shut down. We find alternative strategies to cope. We blame ourselves. We resign ourselves to the painful situation. Like the frog in the slow-boiling pot of water, we're in imminent danger, but even as the water heats up we rationalize away the dire reality of our circumstances. We're created with an extraordinary capacity to disassociate—a gift in certain painful circumstances, but a sentence of soul death for the long run. Like the Israelites, we must awaken to the reality of our circumstances, crying out under the burden with a longing for something better, even if we lack the imagination for it.

It was the groans and cries of God's people that awakened God's rescuing response in the Exodus story (Exodus 2:23-24; 3:7-8). We've got to take the pain seriously, and this story, among many other biblical ones, offers us hope that our cries are heard and held. Of course, for the Israelites and for us, there is no quick fix, no speedy path through a dark wilderness. God offers hope for a day in the distant future (Exodus 3:17), stirring longing and an imagination for a more spacious place of peace and flourishing— a place of shalom.

More often than not, we cry out when we've come to the end of our own resources, when we just can't do it anymore. This is where real transformation begins. Jesus begins his Sermon on the Mount in this place:

> Blessed are the poor in spirit, for theirs is the kingdom of heaven.
> Blessed are those who mourn, for they will be comforted.
> (Matthew 5:3-4)

The one who heals and flourishes often hits bottom first—as Alcoholics Anonymous has taught for decades. The "poor in spirit" are at the end of their rope, and their "mourning" allows them to speak every secret grief out loud, before God and their community, for the sake of healing. As the Beatitudes unfold, the journey appears strikingly similar to the Exodus journey. New longings grow for a better and more just life (Matthew 5:6), shattered hearts become more whole (Matthew 5:8), crucial conversations are engaged (Matthew 5:9), and painful encounters arise along the way (Matthew 5:10-12). But every healing journey begins with a recognition that life in the Egypt that enslaves us is no longer sustainable. The Israelites escaped their terror through bloodshed and plague. The walls were coming down around them even as God paved a way for them. Isn't this the reality of our lives too? If we are courageous enough to confront the toxin of narcissism in our relationships and churches, and brave enough to leave its sinister grip, we too will likely experience the frightening backlash of the Pharaoh-like narcissist. Even after we escape his immediate grip, the psychological grip remains. At times we'll feel compelled to return to the familiar. At other times we may become traumatically frozen in fear of the future. The relief of escaping his immediate grip is often short-lived, as a wilderness of painful growth and transformation awaits ahead.

It's striking to me that on the heels of their escape and at a moment of uncertainty, God chooses to speak a blessing over Israel, calling them his "treasured possession," a "holy nation," and a "priestly kingdom" (Exodus 19:5-6). On the healing journey, it's important to take seriously how you've formed your identity in and through relationship with a narcissist, how this relationship came to enslave you, and how you are being called into a new freedom and identity. God speaks a noble word over a people previously called slaves. I'm reminded often how important it is for traumatized victims to hear a blessing—"you are so courageous," "your hope inspires me," "you deserve so much more."

This blessing is a first taste of new life—lasting shalom. However, it's only as someone gets away from the immediate grip of a narcissist that she realizes the depth of her self-contempt and trauma. The healing journey is about moving from self-contempt to self-love, from shame to self-compassion, from self-reliance to surrendered vulnerability. And yet most victims will tell you that the wilderness gets darker before it gets brighter. The narcissist's grip occupies psychological space. We may leave Egypt, but Egypt lives on in our traumatized psyches. The narcissistic abuser may continue to hold some power—over one's reputation or parenting schedule or financial well-being. Tears of lament are shed for lost years, a lost reputation, lost dignity, lost intimacy, lost vocational stability. Trauma once frozen may begin to seep out in rage or self-deprecating shame. Vacillations of emotions characterize this wilderness season. A lovely oasis moment of peace may be followed by a visitation of profound sadness. It's important to have a reliable wilderness guide in this season—a veteran therapist or spiritual director to walk you through the dark night.

Just as Moses brings the law to Israel, so a wise guide can offer a sense of direction for the journey. The law wasn't given only as a moral guideline but as a path forward: *Go in this way and you'll experience blessing.* It was an invitation to the people of Israel to rearrange their lives according to God's design for flourishing. Those who have been traumatized wonder "How do I do life now?" When a church begins its process of recovery from narcissistic leadership, it is often addicted to old patterns and in need of new pathways. The new path is a cruciform one, requiring us to die to all of the old patterns that squelched life and sabotaged hope. Lesslie Newbigin writes,

> There is no escape from the problem of leadership. . . . The wrong kind of leadership in the Church has played a terrible role in history. . . . Yet we have to insist that the church cannot live its life and fulfill God's purpose for it without leadership. . . . Everything depends upon the pattern of leadership. . . .

Jesus rises from his knees and calls his disciples. "Rise, let us be going," he says, and goes before them—to the Cross. There is the pattern of leadership for the church.[2]

This new pattern is a painful one, a journey through an uncertain wilderness. Every transformational journey assumes a similar pattern. It's essential for us to do the hard work of rooting out the internal and external systemic toxin of traumatic narcissism that remains. A wife can leave a narcissistic abuser. A church can fire a narcissistic pastor. But after this, the real work begins.

As I've said, the work we do in the wilderness phase of our healing journey requires the leadership of a good and wise guide. A therapist and a spiritual director can provide personal guidance in the weeks, months, and years of personal and relational healing. An organizational consultant can guide a church through its own painful wilderness. Robert Quinn, a secular organizational psychologist, uses similar language, saying that an organization must go on a "heroic journey" through a "land of uncertainty" on a path to "deep change."[3] For both individuals and organizations, this is a long journey on which we gain greater awareness of the extent of the trauma, untangle twisted systemic dynamics, heal wounds, lament, and risk vulnerability again. In time an abiding sense of peace will grow within. But we must be patient with ourselves. There is no fixed timetable for this journey.

Finally, on this journey, the promised land isn't a magical place of perpetual cheer but a new space of inner freedom and relational flourishing. Before Jesus returns to make all things new, we experience this freedom in fits and starts. The memory of Egypt fades over time. A new resilience takes root. Faith, hope, and love grow within. There are days that are hard, but there are also days of remarkable peace. We sense God's nearness. We feel inexplicably held. The grip of the old gives way to the grace of the new. Perhaps we even feel an inclination to forgive.

Paul's healing journey took time. In the aftermath of his traumatic encounter with the lead pastor and elder lawyer, he vented to friends, drank too much, and frantically searched for work. When he found a ministry role in the same city I was living in, he came to me for counseling. In our first weeks working together, he spoke of symptoms like insomnia and chronic fatigue, tremors in his hands, paranoia and hypervigilance, feelings of rage, intrusive thoughts, brief flirtations with self-harm, weight gain, alcohol abuse, mood swings, and marital discord. When I asked if anyone else knew of these things, he said, "Why would they? I've got to keep it together. I might get fired again." Paul was no longer working for Bart or at his old church, but Bart's abuse was still alive and well in Paul. He was not yet free from narcissism's traumatic impact on his body.

When we're traumatized, some of us fight. And some of us flee. But trauma theorists tell us that a third response might be the most toxic to our souls—the freeze response. Immobilized by a traumatic situation, we shut down, unable to process the reality of what is happening. Our stunned response might even lead us into a dissociative place, seemingly outside of our own body, self-protected in order to avoid further harm. While animals in the wild have an amazing capacity to process their trauma through organic, bodily means, human evolution may actually work against us on this front, as we're more prone to internalize, disassociate, and disown our trauma in ways that backfire, emerging in painful and lasting symptoms.[4]

Paul's healing journey was hindered by his self-protective strategies and coping mechanisms. But as his symptoms got worse, his wife confronted him. Through tears, Paul told me that he was terribly frightened, all alone, and unsure of what life might look like going forward. He had entered a daunting wilderness. We began the work of processing his traumatic time at the former church, his fear, his sadness, his rage, his experiences of feeling like a little boy, bullied like he had been when he was just eight years old. Along with our work, I referred him to a somatic experiencing therapist, a specialist trained to help the body to fully process frozen trauma.[5] Days turned to weeks and months of work together, and Paul's symptoms faded as hope and resilience and joy slowly returned.

Stacy longed to be strong during her time at seminary. She wanted to prove to herself, to her family members, and to her friends that she could make it in the man's world of a conservative, complementarian seminary. She had learned at an early age, amid a chaotic home, to take care of herself, and took a vow to never, ever back away from a trial. But on an evening before a church history exam with the antagonistic professor, she thought she was having a heart attack and went to the emergency room. In fact, she was having a major panic attack. The ER doctor, a strong, independent woman herself, referred her to a local therapist she trusted. And Stacy's wilderness journey began.

Stacy's Egypt was a seminary system that oppressed, abused, and harassed. Yet she also carried within her the enslaving impact of an abusive childhood. In some ways, she thought she was tough enough to endure this psychological prison. It was a painful moment when, with her therapist, she confessed her fear, her weakness, her powerlessness. Aware of the grip of her inner prison, she now contemplated leaving the outer prison of her seminary, but feelings of failure and shame collapsed like ten-foot waves on her. With her therapist, she decided it might be best to remain enrolled, as she worked to grieve and heal her inner trauma until she felt ready to make a decision to stay or leave from a place of clarity and calm. Through her work, Stacy noticed the symptoms relaxing while a new sense of compassion, even for her classmates and professor, grew. "What pain they must be in," she said. "They are little boys who've become spiritual bullies, and I feel such deep sadness for them and for the church."

Heather's trauma from her marriage, along with unhelpful biblical malpractice offered by her pastor, led to feelings of powerlessness and isolation. Years of enduring Len's abuse took their toll. Her children began to act out in ways that finally led her to get her oldest son into counseling with a veteran marriage and family therapist named Dan. Within five minutes of her debrief with Dan, he said, "So, I'm quite concerned about your son, but I'm very, very concerned about you, Heather." After her initial protestations of "I'm fine" and "I'll be alright," she broke down, shedding tears she'd held for years.

Her own trauma manifested in digestive issues, weight loss, headaches, hypervigilance, sexual anorexia, panic attacks, nightmares, and an overprotective and anxious parenting style. Thankfully, Dan recognized that her son's issues could only be addressed well if Heather's were addressed. Even more, Dan began to make connections to Heather's relationship with her father, another abusive relationship that made for the perfect setup for a relationship with an emotionally immature and unavailable husband.

Heather went on her own healing journey, a journey that Len refused to engage. She stayed with Len during much of this journey, growing in resilience, self-compassion, confidence, and peace. Her symptoms subsided. Her sense of clarity grew. And she began making plans for her future, wisely and reflectively. When Heather was healthy and empowered enough to tell Len that she wanted a separation, she had both the inner and outer resources to handle Len's reaction and her church's moralistic response.[6]

HEALING OURSELVES

A client once said to me, "In every year of our work together, I've taken more and more of my story seriously." She told me that she wouldn't have guessed that we'd spend four years working through what she initially thought to be seasonal depression. I had suspected from the beginning that much more was going on, but that the process of waking up to the depths of pain and trauma could not be sped up for the sake of therapeutic efficiency.

Amid the busyness of our lives, who among us has the time or energy to mine the depths of our stories? My answer is, who among us can afford to neglect our story? I lament the reality that many of us, myself included, find ourselves too busy, too habituated to the demands of modern life, too out of touch with deeper emotions, to take our stories seriously and to embark on a healing journey. Indeed, some will suggest that it's selfish or even narcissistic to do this work.

Healing requires radical honesty with ourselves and the courage to follow through on the wilderness path. Perhaps the two most important components of healing trauma are *awareness* and *intentionality*. Because trauma thrives in the shadows, awareness and intentionality are often neglected for self-protection, disconnection, and self-sabotage. Memories may be repressed, bodily sensations ignored, and feelings and needs disregarded. Anyone serious about healing enters into a journey in which habitual patterns of disconnection and disregard are addressed, and new pathways forged.

Heather's healing journey didn't begin for a long time because she was in a marriage and in an ecclesial system that demanded she disregard her feelings and needs. This was her Egypt. Her abuse was not only emotional but spiritual, and her journey of growing awareness and intentional engagement led to a myriad of complex emotions. At first, she was reluctant, doubting the reality of her perceptions, prone to think that if she'd just have more faith or be a more devoted wife, things would change. She worked hard to clean up her prison cell, but to no avail.

Indeed, many of us choose the predictable pain of our own Egypts over the risky, vulnerable path of the wilderness. This is why it's hard to go on this journey alone. Wise guides who've navigated the terrain before can help us see our strategies, our symptoms, our ways of coping. They speak words of blessing and hold us in times of anxiety and resignation. Stacy's therapist provided a safe place in a world of judgment and abuse. As Paul's therapist and spiritual director, I invited him to relinquish addictive coping patterns and feel the sadness, the shame, and the loss that came from his traumatic experience with Bart. When Heather went forward with her separation from Dan, she was inundated by people from the church who wanted to have coffee, so-called friends who told her that "every marriage has problems" or "the Lord can't reconcile this" or "maybe you're just blowing it out of proportion." Her therapist helped her share her story selectively and wisely, trusting only a few with her most vulnerable self.

Every healing journey is unique. There is no clear roadmap that names all the roadblocks, detours, and obstacles along the way. One of my former clients would often say as she was leaving my office, "I just need to trust the process, right?" We long to control and strategize a journey that can only unfold in its own time. We long to heal ourselves, but Jesus says, "Come to me, all you that are weary and are carrying heavy burdens, and I will give you rest" (Matthew 11:28). In the end, we must go. Recall Newbigin's perspective that we explored earlier in this chapter: "Jesus rises from his knees and calls his disciples. 'Rise, let us be going,' he says, and goes before them—to the Cross. There is the pattern of leadership for the church."

HEALING THE CHURCH

The church that fired Paul was led by Bart, a narcissistic leader who, as one former staff member said, "left a trail of dead bodies in his wake." Evading accountability for years, Bart hid behind the successful growth of his church, the appeal of his Sunday morning teachings, and a compelling social media platform.

Several years after Paul was fired, another former staff member reached out, sharing with Paul that Bart had been fired himself. Paul was asked to join a group of eight former staff in a space where they could tell their stories to the leadership council of the church. Tears streamed from Paul's eyes as he felt a sense of validation and experienced an invitation to once and for all tell his story.

In the aftermath of Bart's termination, the remaining team of pastors and leaders were traumatized and scared. There was no apparent successor. Bart fired most of the talented leaders before they could threaten him, and those who remained were mostly passive, compliant, and fearful. The church's leadership council was unprepared for this moment too, but in their anxiety they reached out to a veteran organizational psychologist and former pastor, a wise and important decision that altered the course of their church.

The organizational psychologist meticulously brought order to the chaos. Like Moses at Sinai, he realized that the church was living in the chaos of an Egypt and needed a path forward, a way of flourishing, a reordering of life together. As with individuals, churches must engage in a process of healing with awareness and intentionality. Too often a church damaged by a narcissistic leader will languish in the aftermath, paralyzed by anxiety or addicted to old patterns of leading and relating that only bring more mistrust and harm. As we saw in chapter six, systems infected with the toxin of narcissism are traumatized in ways similar to traumatized individuals. Systems can experience immobilization, unhealthy reactivity, and continued addictions to unhealth. Removing a toxic leader does not heal an infected system. It may even shine a greater light on the systemic unhealth.

Paul's former church was wise to bring in an experienced veteran of ministry and dysfunctional systems. Each church healing journey is different, but I've rarely seen a healthy recovery happen without a wise guide accompanying and leading it. Too often the remaining members in the church and leadership are too affected by the system's dynamics to foster meaningful change. Churches that long to heal do well to hire a consultant with expertise and experience. In this case, the outside consultant took the leadership council and church on a year-long journey in three phases.

Phase one was a season of truth-telling. By creating spaces for dialogue, the organizational psychologist stewarded a process of honesty and transparency, which led to difficult conversations and significant disagreements about Bart's leadership and its impact. She carefully cultivated respectful encounters, even among those who disagreed, emphasizing the need to listen and understand rather than agree or disagree. Phase one took several months. No major changes were made, and the church committed to a season of simplicity in ministry. There were times of grief and lament, sprinkled with glimpses of hope. Some impatient folks left the church, unhappy with the process or disgruntled that Bart had been fired. This can be expected. A good consultant is able to weather uncertainty and storms that arise during this initial season.

After several months of self-examination, the consultant asked the remaining leaders if they were ready to enter into a second phase in which they'd reimagine their sense of call, mission, and identity. Most remaining staff members were eager for the next phase, but a bit too eager to make big decisions about leadership structures and a new lead pastor. Anxiety often propels teams into reactive rather than reflective processes. But in this next phase, the consultant led intentional conversations about their longings for the church and its flourishing. Staff and leadership council members started experiencing deepening trust and connection with one another as larger desires and longings were shared, sometimes through tears. She'd point out resonances she was hearing. They'd write these themes on a white board and return to these themes time and again to see if a collective consensus was emerging. People felt empowered, excited, and hopeful.

By the end of the second phase, many who remained in these visionary conversations sensed that a final phase was emerging. The consultant told them that phase three meant that her time of leadership would gradually come to a close. Yet, because of their newfound empowerment and confidence, the team felt confident that it would be okay, even without their wise guide holding their hand. They would need to own this next season of restructuring, while stewarding a process in which they'd hire their next lead pastor. Together they had grieved a painful past. Together they reimagined a healthier vision of life together for the future. Together they articulated a clear description and profile for their next pastor. Together they identified new roles and healthy authority structures within the organization, this time chosen by them and not dictated to them. They were collectively empowered, and their trust for one another allowed them to step courageously into their final task.

Most were surprised by their growing resilience as individuals and as a team. In a final meeting, which included staff and the remaining leadership council members, they took time to reflect on their year, offering gratitude to one another and reflections on what they'd learned. Most remembered their anger and hopelessness of a year ago, expressing thanks that a journey through a grief-filled wilderness had led to growing hope and trust. Some expressed what they saw growing in others, including previously unseen gifts and emerging confidence that inspired the team.

The work they'd done assured that the next pastor would be a healthy, collaborative leader—and that's who they hired. Because of their diligent work, they were able to navigate the storm of leadership transition. Even more, they were able to die to old, unhealthy patterns of life together and discover new, healthy ones. The church itself changed in marked ways, leading dozens if not hundreds to leave. But those who remained were deeply invested in what was emerging, and they had matured through the wilderness season.

The healing journey isn't painless, for individuals or for congregations. Band-aid remedies may stop the bleeding temporarily, but those invested in real change will engage the trauma intentionally and seek wise guides to direct them along the way.

FURTHER RESOURCES

Robert Quinn. *Deep Change: Discovering the Leader Within*. San Francisco: Jossey-Bass, 1996.

Chuck DeGroat. *Leaving Egypt: Finding God in the Wilderness Places*. Grand Rapids: Faith Alive Christian Resources, 2011.

Jim Herrington and Trisha Taylor. *Learning Change: Congregational Transformation Fueled by Personal Renewal*. Grand Rapids: Kregel, 2017.

CHAPTER NINE

TRANSFORMATION FOR NARCISSISTS (IS POSSIBLE)

True peace will come only when every individual finds peace within themselves, when we have all vanquished and transformed our hatred for our fellow human beings into·love one day.

ETTY HILLESUM

O ne of the hardest things about writing a book on narcissism, and thus on narcissists, is the reduction of a human soul to a label. In this book and in my prior writing, I've tried to honor the complexity of human beings. I've often said that each of us is both beautiful *and* broken, hiding *and* hidden in Christ, knowable *and* utterly mysterious. The late philosopher-poet John O'Donohue paints a lovely picture of this mystery: "There is a desire in many people in the modern world to see themselves clearly. But if you listen to them, between the psychological clichés and the chatter of false intimacy, what they're seeing is a certain limited image that they have partly projected and partly excavated, but which is terribly limited in proportion to the vast immensity that's actually within them."[1] O'Donohue's words are humbling, for even the most self-excavated among us only sees through a mirror dimly. Even if we can define and categorize our pathologies, our Enneagram habits, or our Myers-Briggs types, we are still blind to significant spaces in our soul.

O'Donohue reminds me that while there is arrogance and certainty in the habitual patterns of a narcissist, there is also arrogance in presuming that a pathological definition says everything that there is to say about someone. He also hints at one of the keys to transformation—awakening to the extraordinary reality that you are more than your diagnosis, more than your addiction, more than your personality type, more than a psychological definition.

But I like definitions. I like categories. They give me a sense of control. When a student tells me he's an Enneagram One, I whisper to myself, "That's why he's so perfectionistic." When a client tells me her psychiatrist diagnosed her with bipolar, I think, "Oh good. Now we know what's really going on." I confess that it's easier to have a box to put someone in or a label to define someone with.

I like definitions because I'm busy and I don't have time to traverse the expansive territory of the soul. It's especially helpful in my busy and anxious world, where I need to be efficient, where wading into O'Donohue's "vast immensity" feels too messy and too time consuming.

I like definitions because they give me a sense of power. If you've abused your spouse, manipulated friends, lied to cover it up, and smiled all the way through it, it helps me to label you a narcissist. I confess this, as each and every therapist should, because we're not passionless robots. We get angry. We seethe at injustice. And our expertise at labeling provides us with a needed sense of power.

I like definitions because I'm a fixer. While I say in these pages that the soul is vast and complex, and while I believe to my core that the real treasure and the real pain in each one of us exists beneath the mysterious waterline, I secretly want to fix, to tinker. I secretly believe that if I know what's wrong, I can solve the problem.

I like definitions because living in binaries is easier. It's easier to slice the world into bad and good, redeemed and unredeemed, righteous and wicked, victim and abuser. However, as the fourth-century desert father Macarius said beautifully,

> Within the heart are unfathomable depths. There are reception rooms and bedchambers in it, doors and porches, and many offices and passages. In it is the workshop of righteousness and of wickedness. In it is death; in it is life. The heart is Christ's palace: there Christ the King comes to take his rest, with the angels and spirits of the saints, and he dwells there, walking within it and placing his Kingdom there. The heart is but a small vessel: and yet dragons and lions are there, and there poisonous creatures and all the treasures of wickedness; rough uneven places are there, and gaping chasms. There likewise is God, there are the angels, there life and the Kingdom, there light and the apostles, the heavenly cities and the treasures of grace. All things are there.[2]

We are complex, a vast immensity, a mystery to ourselves, known only and ultimately by a God who seems fearless in the face of our complexity, capable of loving each of us and all of us in our beauty and brokenness. And because of this, I can believe that someone who has been diagnosed as narcissistic is seen and known to his depths by a God who refuses to reduce anyone to a label, who both confronts sin with an utter seriousness and offers grace with utter lavishness.

So each time I sit with someone who is narcissistic, I confess. I remind myself that she is one who has hurt others deeply *and* one who is created in God's image. I confess my need to define and control, and I ask for eyes to see and ears to hear a story much larger and to believe a redemption far greater.

This began for me in the early 2000s, when I was counseling Shane. Shane's prior therapist confronted him with his narcissistic patterns. During their time of counseling with this therapist, his wife, Gretchen, courageously named his arrogance, emotional abuse, financial foul play, and other damaging relational patterns. But something odd happened during this season. During one of their sessions, the therapist pulled out a Bible, held it up in a dramatic display, and looked squarely at Gretchen saying, "He is the definition of a wicked man, a man without hope. Wicked men don't change." Hearing this, Gretchen broke into hopeless tears. Shane stared down at the floor—a man sentenced and convicted. When they left the session, Gretchen walked out and said to Shane, "If it's hopeless and you can't change, I want a divorce." Shane simmered with quiet rage, his teeth clenched, shaking his head in disbelief, resigned to his sentence.

Is the final verdict on Shane that "wicked men don't change"? Or is there hope? A pathway of transformation requires us to honor O'Donohue's wise words as we both define a reality and recognize that the definition does not represent all of who Shane is. When Shane came to see me for counseling, he was anxious and reticent, defensive and unpliable, awaiting my judgment. He was certain he was not a narcissist and he was there to prove it. And so I tried something with him I wasn't sure would work. I asked him if he would be willing to explore the possibility that his relational patterns were narcissistic and hurtful if I wouldn't see this as the final word on his character and person. He seemed surprised, sitting silently. Then after a minute or two—and through tears—he said, "Deal."

THE GRAND BARGAIN

Do you remember the old television show *Let's Make a Deal*, hosted by Monte Hall? Contestants could choose one of three curtains, with the possibility that one might reveal a great prize and another a silly consolation. At times Hall would offer the chance for smaller prizes with higher odds, enticing the contestants to choose between good and even better.

It's the game of life. We're all always choosing in all sorts of ways. Do I want to take the reliable route to the gym or the quicker Thirty-Second-Street route with the risk being delayed by a train? Will I choose the safe choice of the burger at the brewery or risk today's "special"?

As I've counseled men and women who are diagnosably narcissistic, I've found that this approach is a helpful path forward in our work. There have been times I've played hardball, assuming the role of the tough, confrontational therapist. There have been times I've played the good cop, buddying up in an attempt to win trust. My naive attempts to break through have helped at times, but I've often run into dead ends. I've learned that honesty is better than some therapeutic posture.

Over the years, doing this work has also cured me of my binary posture toward complex human beings. In my book *Wholeheartedness,* I introduce a therapeutic paradigm called "internal family systems" (IFS), which values human complexity and provides a pathway for doing transformational work.[3] IFS posits that each of us is both a self and selves, that a core true self is also accompanied by a host of smaller selves—parts of us that may protect us, or cope addictively, or hide, or hold shame, or act playfully. It's a paradigm that hearkens back to the wisdom of Macarius and reminds us that there are chambers in our being that hold beauty and pain, dragons and princesses, angels and devils.

When I began my work with Shane, I didn't yet have this paradigm. But I had an intuition. Romans 7 was percolating in the back of my mind:

I do not understand my own actions. For I do not do what I want, but I do the very thing I hate. Now if I do what I do not want, I agree that the law is good. But in fact it is no longer I that do it, but sin that dwells within me. For I know that nothing good dwells within me, that is, in my flesh. I can will what is right, but I cannot do it. For I do not do the good I want, but the evil I do not want is what I do. Now if I do what I do not want, it is no longer I that do it, but sin that dwells within me. (Romans 7:15-20)

I wanted to believe that Shane's narcissism wasn't the final word on him, but I didn't want to let him off the hook either.

Something akin to this kind of "deal" happens in Susan Howatch's novel *Glittering Images*. In the story, Charles Ashworth is a conflicted Anglican priest and canon theologian who meets with Jon Darrow, a keen spiritual director who confronts Ashworth's false self—what he calls his "glittering image." Darrow does something remarkable. He speaks directly to the "glittering" part of Ashworth saying,

"He must be exhausted. Has he never been tempted to set down the burden by telling someone about it?"

"I can't," Ashworth replies.

"Who's 'I'?" said Darrow.

"The glittering image."

"Ah yes," said Darrow, "and of course that's the only Charles Ashworth that the world's allowed to see, but you're out of the world now, aren't you, and I'm different from everyone else because I know there are two of you. I'm becoming interested in this other self of yours, the self nobody meets. I'd like to help him come out from behind that glittering image and set down this appalling burden which has been tormenting him for so long."

"He can't come out."

"Why not?"

"You wouldn't like or approve of him."

"Charles, when a traveler's staggering along with a back-breaking amount of luggage he doesn't need someone to pat him on the head and tell him how wonderful he is. He needs someone who'll offer to share the load."[4]

I love this exchange because Darrow, the wise spiritual director, refuses to believe that Ashworth is the sum of his narcissistic traits. In much the same way, I presented Shane with a third way, beyond confrontation and collusion. I offered him a deal, of sorts. I asked him to trust me to engage the most toxic aspects of his personality while at the same time believing the best about him. I told him that I wouldn't and couldn't do this work unless I believed that there was deep goodness and beauty in every soul, that I wouldn't and couldn't plumb the depths if I didn't think I'd find treasure. Shane relaxed just a bit, enough for us to get started. I think that he secretly hoped that we might be able to find some of that illusive treasure.

This "third way" has been among the most helpful and hopeful pathways to transformation among those I've worked with. It neither exonerates nor condemns. It holds both beauty and brokenness. It admits complexity. It invites curiosity.

DON'T SPLIT ON ME

Shane was one of the most willing and cooperative narcissistic clients I've ever seen. I won't pretend that each case proceeds so collaboratively. Narcissists are trapped in a psychic bondage, a phenomenon psychologists call "splitting"—an incapacity to integrate the shadow and the light, the good and the bad, the beauty and the brokenness.[5] They are often so defended against the shadow aspects of their being that they live out of an unrealistic, idealized version of themselves that they project onto the world. This leads some psychological experts to the conclusion that NPD is treatable but not curable, and some Christians to the conclusion that narcissism is simply wickedness.

I think this is unfortunate. To be sure, the psychic wounds of someone with NPD are profound and their wall of armor is thick, but my deep conviction is that buried within the most well-defended person is light, glory, dignity, and beauty—the image of God.

This defensiveness is the great obstacle to transformation. For Shane and others like him, change isn't a simple matter of cosmetics—coverup in the form of a shallow repentance, an empty promise to do better, a version of fauxnerability. Transformation requires a journey inward, down into the depths, where both demons and angels lurk. Splitting cuts one off from the possibility of deep exploration.

The good boy and the bad boy within need to befriend one another. We are never either one or the other, but always a mysterious mixture of both. If I live naively unaware of my shadow side, I live disconnected from a vast storehouse of riches that can be discovered only when I befriend my shame, my loneliness, my disappointments, my addictive habits, my secret resentments, my hidden rage.

I am not diagnosably NPD, but even so, when I was first introduced to inner work myself, my fear of being "found out" kept me from fully engaging. The positive narrative I was writing for myself was of a young seminarian getting top grades, invitations to study further abroad, exciting opportunities to do ministry internationally. The future looked really good. And so I felt like the psychological work I was being asked to do threatened my inner "good boy," including my good standing among peers and colleagues and the promise of ministry success. What if what I discovered threatened my good standing?

In reality, my unawareness left me blind to the real effects of my actions. While my inner narrative was positive, I soon discovered that female peers at the seminary experienced me as arrogant and dismissive. My wife experienced me as moody and emotionally manipulative. In other words, my unexplored shadow side was finding an outlet, despite my defensive repression of it. And my own narcissistic self-image took a hit when I discovered my negative impact on others. I had a choice to make.

In reality, we all have a choice to make. Splitting is a common phenomenon. The healthier folks among us are simply aware that they are doing it, and their awareness allows them to hold the good, the bad, and the ugly before God in a posture of humble surrender, grief, and repentance. For a narcissist, the real transformational work begins when he enters into the inner conversation in earnest. Such a conversation opens up the possibility both of radical honesty with himself and with those who experience narcissism's bite.

HOW DO YOU EXPERIENCE ME?

When I teach on the dynamics of real change and maturation, I often describe a "furnace of transformation" each of us must pass through for the sake of growth and refinement. I've never seen real growth occur without suffering, humiliation, disappointment, and pain. The way of transformation is the way of the cross, a journey in which our sufferings make a way for resurrection (Philippians 3:7-11).

It often takes an honest and sometimes painful relational encounter to prompt this transformational journey. A pastor named Mark discovered this in an exercise we did with his staff. Mark's narcissism created an organizational church system filled with anxiety, resentment, and a fair amount of terror. When my good friend and I were called in to consult by Mark's exasperated elder board, we saw in Mark a pastor whose self-awareness was extremely low. Though a charismatic, articulate, thirtysomething pastor, he had little idea of his impact on others. His church plant had grown quickly, and as it had, he'd hired staff at a frenetic pace—but he'd never before led a staff of even a few people. He was so terrified of being exposed as incompetent that at one point he threatened to quit if the elders sought outside counsel.

But he didn't quit. In a phone call, I shared with him my perspective. I said, "Mark, you're obviously gifted. But I sense that there's a you so few know, a part of you hidden behind the polished self that speaks every Sunday morning, a part of you that feels lonely at times, maybe in over his head at other times." His curiosity grew in this conversation, as he took the risk of believing that I might actually be *for* him.

And then I asked him if he'd be willing to do something really hard: "Mark, would you be willing to sit down with some of your senior leaders on staff one-on-one along with me and ask a hard question?"

He listened with curiosity.

And then he started to negotiate the rules of engagement.

After a few minutes, I said, "Mark, this isn't a trial! It's simply an act of humility. I am inviting you to ask a question: How do you experience me?"

He wrangled and slithered, wondering if he'd be able to respond after they spoke and curious about what I'd do with the information. He was split, defending the good boy at all costs, and perhaps terrified by what might happen within and amidst his staff if he dared to open conversation to the bad boy inside of him. In the end, he agreed reluctantly, most likely because his job and public reputation might have been in jeopardy if he resisted the elder-mandated process.

Because of this external, vocational threat, I worried that Mark might not be relaxed and surrendered enough to humbly engage the process. But we went ahead. Staff members came before him one by one, and he asked them, "How do you experience me?" And each time, he heard strikingly similar accounts.

Unpredictable. Angry. Demanding. Gifted. Inspiring. Confusing. Arrogant. Defensive. Visionary. Risk-taking. Hopeful. Exasperating. Unrealistic. Frenetic. Energetic. Frightening.

The mirror was held before Mark, and as each staff member came and went, Mark's spirit grew heavier and soberer. At times, he attempted to apologize. At other times, he wanted to respond defensively but bit his tongue. In the end, we sat for an hour to debrief. I asked him, "What if all of those things are you? What if you're gifted *and* hurtful, inspiring *and* terrifying?"

The most important moment in the furnace came when I sat down with Mark and his wife, Shawna. Shawna was the champion, a stalwart defender of her oft-abused and maligned husband. I sensed that Shawna's honest participation in this process might make it or break it. Often when a spouse defends the narcissistic false self with the same ferocity as the narcissist himself (or herself), there's little chance of traversing the transformative path.

But Shawna dared to agree with the assessment of Mark's staff colleagues. Through tears, she said she was terrified to do so. In fact, she said something that stoked the furnace's fire even hotter. She said, "Mark, I'm frightened you'll kill yourself because of this." As it turns out, Shawna had lived their nine years of marriage protecting Mark's fragile false self because of her fear of his issues of depression, addiction, and self-contempt. She was betting on

Mark's success as a way of keeping him protected from his lurking shadow side.

He looked at her with disgust and rage. She'd named a secret self he preferred to keep locked inside a vault within. And she looked at him, shaking her head, saying, "I love you. I'm not going anywhere." They simultaneously burst into tears, holding one another, and tears streamed down my face too. Mark's transformational journey was just beginning. He'd faced the hardest question he ever had to answer: How do you experience me?

THE SLOW REVEAL

I love home makeover shows with "big reveals." It all began with a show from many years ago—*Trading Spaces*. And then came *Extreme Makeover: Home Edition*, *Love It or List It*, *Fixer Upper*, and more. I don't watch them religiously, but I'll admit a fascination for makeover stories. At times, the transformations move me to tears. At their best, these shows tell stories of brokenness and beauty.

Working with narcissists, I'm not afforded "big reveals." What I do experience is what I call the "slow reveal." Stories of transformation cannot be squeezed into half-hour shows or cooked in psychological microwaves. Self-revelation isn't complete after one aha moment before a therapist. It's not complete after a good cry and hugs of love and forgiveness.

I was reminded of this recently when I received a letter from a man I counseled in Orlando. My journey in ministry has taken me from Orlando to San Francisco to Holland, Michigan, and I have a storehouse of memories from encounters in offices and coffee shops and living rooms in each of these places. So when I saw this man's name I remembered distinctly the office we met in, the lovely aesthetic of the room, the dim lights—and the brutal early encounters we experienced.

I had been a young therapist. In my anxiety, my approach had been more confrontational, and he defended himself well. Sadly, I was mostly unhelpful to him, except that "no man has ever dared say the hard things you said that winter we worked together," as he wrote. I was humbled to hear him renarrate a situation I recalled as a personal failure. I was also moved by his recounting of the next decade of work he did.

He was reading blogs I'd been writing on narcissism, and he saw aspects of himself in a few of the stories I was offering. He wrote to let me know there was hope—that he himself was an example of hope. He spoke of an "excruciatingly slow" process, which required him to take time away from ministry and relinquish his ordination in the denomination he'd first been ordained within. He shared the humiliation of working part-time jobs around town and seeing former parishioners who wondered why he disappeared. He spoke of the hard work he and his spouse were doing in counseling and noted that it had taken years for her to trust again—and even to sleep in the same bed again. He was now just beginning the process of reentering pastoral ministry.

His was a slow reveal.

Indeed, every transformational journey is a long and winding wilderness road.

Too often, however, I see women and men I counsel resist this, sabotaging the possibility of growth as they return to the old, worn patterns that seemed to work before. One pastor I worked with said, "I simply can't afford a season of humiliation." Well defended, he rolled the dice, hoping he could survive the questions being raised about his leadership and character.

There are varying reasons for this resistance. There are external factors. If she does the hard work of slow-cook transformation, she may lose standing in her community, lose the book deal, risk losing a loyal following, or become the target of suspicion or judgment. In my work, the external factors can be quite powerful obstacles to honest engagement. Sometimes a faction of devoted followers will pledge their loyalty in a way that provides the necessary fuel to resist. Sometimes a loyal, colluding spouse can get in the way of a narcissist's self-revelation. Sometimes church leadership teams protect the narcissist for fear of what might happen if his leadership is lost.

Even more powerful, however, are the internal factors. Narcissists have well-defended parts of themselves that they simply refuse to surrender. In a single counseling session, I can often see the subtle changes in a client as she negotiates the cost of surrender. I think of a woman whose eyes were soft and tearful as we talked about how fragile and vulnerable she felt as a little girl. In those few moments, she offered me the rarest of glimpses into a part of her that few had ever seen or known. But within moments, her jaw clenched, her eyes glazed in anger, and she looked on me as her abuser. Surrender had turned to suspicion, and I sensed hope slipping away as she recommitted to never, ever letting anyone get close and hurt her again. Even today, she is still viewed by many as a bully. What happened to that soft, vulnerable little girl that required such significant self-protection?

These inner resistances are parts of a psychic fortress that protects against further abuse or abandonment or rejection or humiliation. A bullied and broken little boy named Adolf becomes a vicious terrorist. This is not an excuse nor a reason to let a brutal dictator like Hitler, or even a bullying pastor, off the hook. Indeed, it highlights even more the extraordinary obstacles to transformation and raises the stakes for those of us who long to be agents of both justice and healing. We are working against outer and inner resistances that conspire to sabotage repentance and healing, and so our approach must be wise.

My early vacillation between combative and passive approaches only served to reinforce the resistances of my clients. In truth, I wanted an approach that would get a result, rather than entering wisely into a slow growth process that might unfold in fits and starts. I was too eager to oversimplify. I wasn't ready or equipped to enter the long, painstaking battle for the soul's freedom. The slow reveal manifests over years rather than days, amid resistance and sabotage. Those who work with narcissists and hope for transformation must be ready to endure losses in minor battles for the sake of a larger war for the soul. And while I don't love combat imagery as a metaphor, I do think it is appropriate, given the inner war within the conflicted psyche of a narcissist. Indeed, I have to be ready to lose along the way. As a therapist, or a friend, or a spouse, I ought to be ready for significant disappointments, and be mindful that hopelessness and resignation will arise within me time and again. If we are committed to the process of transformation, extraordinary patience will be required of us.

THE ONLY SOLUTION

I'm often asked how I'm able to do this work, and why I'd want to. The answer is simple—I'm a glutton for redemption stories. Something in me refuses to give up on any human being. On one hand, I experience disgust at the pain narcissists inflict, sometimes in ways that do significant damage to the souls of others. I've encountered it myself. My own livelihood and reputation were jeopardized. I fell into depression and severe anxiety. I longed for revenge. There were days when rage felt like my best friend.

But over time, and under no compulsion, a growing sense of compassion welled up within me. I no longer felt the need to bathe my pain under the label of victim. I began to see the one who hurt me as one who was hurt. Interestingly, this manifested in a season of my own therapy in which I began opening up to my own inner complexity—my own dark dragons lurking in the shadows. Somehow, being opened to my own contradictions opened space for the contradictions of others. My own slow reveal allowed for a growing compassion for another.

I'm inspired by Etty Hillesum, the Dutch Jew whose journey of inner healing allowed her to grow into a generous and hospitable woman. Although she had an opportunity to escape Auschwitz, she chose solidarity with her family and friends and was ultimately murdered during the awful mass extinguishment of life suffered by so many during that brutal time. She moved toward the suffering because she no longer lived in an "I'm good, you're bad" universe—she'd become acquainted with her own inner angels and demons, dragons and princesses. Self-compassion led to compassion for the other, including her captors.

In her journal, Etty wrote, "If you have a rich inner life . . . there probably isn't all that much difference between the inside and outside of a camp."[6] She shows a remarkable capacity to allow an inner sense of identity and security in God determine her attitude toward all that arises, both within and outside of her. Even more, she says, "True peace will come only when every individual finds peace within themselves . . . when we have all vanquished and transformed our hatred for our fellow human brings into love one day. Perhaps that is asking too much, but it is, however, the only solution."[7] In this fascinating word play, she proposes love as the "only solution," even as the Nazi "final solution" threatened to extinguish the existence of her people. Patrick Woodhouse writes of Hillesum,

> She never gave up in the hope of seeing—across the chasms of war—the face of the other who is human too. Like us, they

too, are bearers of the Divine image however deeply marred and buried it may be, and so they are people to whom we belong. To remove from the mind the label of "enemy" is like removing the blinds from a window and letting the light in. If you will not hate them, then you may begin to see them. Those who wish to destroy you are human beings.[8]

I wrestle with Etty's gracious "solution," not least because of my own wounds. I've seen narcissists inflict pain, sometimes shamelessly and with a cruelty that shows utter disregard for the souls they are harming. But I never, ever want to become a mirror image of this cruelty. If you are in relationship with a narcissist, whether a spouse or a staff member, a therapist or a pastor, you must be relentlessly committed to doing your own inner work, both to protect yourself and others from harm and to engage from a place of centered compassion rather than reactive rage. If we cannot do this, it's better to step away. Engaging from a place of pain will only multiply the pain.

In the end, the hope of transformation is anchored in the presence of a God who is utterly familiar with all the dark and light within us—and is not afraid of it. Recall the words of Macarius from earlier, "The heart is Christ's palace: there Christ the King comes to take his rest, with the angels and spirits of the saints, and he dwells there, walking within it and placing his Kingdom there." Only the one who allows God to expose the darkness and the light will experience the king's compassion and healing presence.

Transformation is possible. Those hijacked by narcissistic false selves are living in slavery, and in turn they enslave others. But I hold a deep and abiding hope that an Exodus journey is possible for each of us. Some will resist, and the walls of the hell they've chosen will crush them. But there is a transformational journey to take—albeit an arduous one—and a land flowing with milk and honey in the distance.

FURTHER RESOURCES

L. Gregory Jones. *Embodying Forgiveness: A Theological Analysis*. Grand Rapids: Eerdmans, 1995.

Richard Rohr and Paula D'Arcy. *A Spirituality for the Two Halves of Life*. Audio recording. Franciscan Media, 2004.

Patrick Woodhouse. *Etty Hillesum: A Life Transformed*. New York: Continuum, 2009.

EPILOGUE

He Humbled Himself...

W e began this book with an image of Christ's kenosis, his self-emptying, the most profound act of humble surrender and relinquishment, in which Christ,

> who, though he was in the form of God,
> did not regard equality with God
> as something to be exploited,
> but emptied himself,
> taking the form of a slave,
> being born in human likeness.
> And being found in human form,
> he humbled himself
> and became obedient to the point of death—
> even death on a cross. (Philippians 2:5-11)

Though he sat at the right hand of the father, with access and power, Christ willingly abnegated his position to become one of us—fully human, subject to the trauma of childhood rejection, to the mockery of peers, to the ache of a distant father, to the confusion of puberty. "He did not regard equality with God as something to be exploited," Paul says.

God the Son, among us, one of us—and yet he pursued a path so different than the path of exploitative power seen in Herod or Caesar or the Zealots, so unlike the path of certainty and control seen in the Pharisees, so far from the path of upward mobility and success my culture demands. When the crowds came, Jesus didn't stick around long (Matthew 5:1). He'd do miraculous things and say, "Tell no one about this." Offered the kingdoms of the world, he rejected them outright (Matthew 4:1-11). His was a radically humble, self-giving way.

And yet we swim in the waters of narcissism. We are witnesses to power that exploits, deceives, manipulates, coerces, and abuses. Political personalities compete in the arena of Twitter in an age in which scathing indictments of the character of a rival is sport. Meanwhile, stories of abuse and coverup plague the church. Celebrity evangelical pastors face unceremonious falls from power while former celebrities scheme premature comebacks. It's hard to know who to trust. I hear stories regularly about the rural pastor caught in multiple affairs, the multisite leader abusing his staff, the institutional leader covering up the institution's history of racism and sexism. I'm disheartened when a theology of grace is misappropriated by those who've abused power, manipulated the truth, and exploited the powerless. Grace never whitewashes abuse. Grace exposes the abuser, not to shame him but for the sake of truth and healing for all.

For the apostle Paul, the humble, nonexploitative path of Jesus is the pattern for all human relationships:

> Therefore if you have any encouragement from being united with Christ, if any comfort from his love, if any common sharing in the Spirit, if any tenderness and compassion, then make my joy complete by being like-minded, having

the same love, being one in spirit and of one mind. Do nothing out of selfish ambition or vain conceit. Rather, in humility value others above yourselves, not looking to your own
interests but each of you to the interests of the others. In
your relationships with one another, have the same mindset
as Christ Jesus. (Philippians 2:1-5 NIV)

The relational posture of a Christian is anchored in our union with
Christ. God dwells in us, by the Spirit, nearer to us than our very
breath. Anyone who lives from this depth of intimate relationship
will long to be like-minded, unified, unselfish, humble, deferential,
and self-sacrificial—anything but narcissistic. Indeed, this is our
original design, imprinted deep on our being, even prior to our
anxious grasping for other, substitute unions, other "programs
for happiness," as Thomas Keating says.[1] It's what we most deeply
long for, even if our behavior defies it.

The incarnation retunes our anxious and grasping souls,
reminds us of our divine design, and reunites us with our divine
center. Jesus is the living antidote to narcissism. He enters into
the waters of narcissism, suffers in the waters of narcissism, is
crucified in the waters of narcissism, and yet rises through the
waters to redeem and restore the entire cosmos. Jesus makes
possible the redemption of an arrogant murderer and antagonist
who becomes the "apostle to the Gentiles." It's striking to me that
the apostle Paul, whose story is one of remarkable transformation,
can't narrate the pathway of redemption and transformation
without placing the incarnation of Jesus at the very center.[2]

The life of Jesus is the life dynamically alive in us, and yet we
seem to live not from our deep, true self but from contingent
selves, the masks that work for a season but ultimately rob us
of joy and hope. And yet we're invited, with Jesus, to humble

ourselves. We are invited to lay down the masks that protect and defend and to enter vulnerably into union and communion with one another. This was Paul's hope. This is my hope.

I cannot live from this place of depth and union unless I'm willing to see myself clearly, to see the narcissist who lurks within me. Having worked with diagnosably narcissistic women and men for twenty years, I'm more mindful of my own profoundly self-protective strategies. I realize that while I may not spike on the narcissistic spectrum on a psychological test, I am not immune to grandiosity, exploitation, manipulation, absence of empathy, and evasion of my true self, anchored in God-union. I've come to realize that I cannot help *them* until I see myself clearly, until I move with compassion to wounded, weary, and wary parts of me that seem to live more loudly than my true self.

We swim in the waters of narcissism. This means that each of us participates, albeit unwittingly much of the time, in systems and patterns of toxic relating. A scan of the evening news shines a light on our patterns of violence, exploitation, and coercion. Scrolling through Twitter reminds me of just how certain we think we are, quick to condemn, even to shame, another. And yet, scanning my day during an evening practice of the Ignatian Examen reveals my bitter envy of others I see as more important than me, my fear of being misunderstood or becoming irrelevant, my habits of attention seeking and control. I recognize that the healing I most long for in my community and culture might begin with my own humiliation.

In the months it took to write this book, I received quite a bit of affirmation, particularly from those who see this cultural moment as ripe for a book like this. Some took the opportunity to name the current president and political leaders, others a pastor, some a spouse or a close friend. Many are hoping for a roadmap for how to deal with narcissists in their lives. The majority see narcissism as a problem "out there" to be solved by clinicians and technicians of the soul.

As I conclude my writing, I wonder whether this book will be of any help, particularly if the reader remains unwilling to explore his or her own narcissism. How can we address the wounds in others if we are unwilling to address our own? Can we even begin to live into Paul's vision of community if only some of us are the problem?

The danger of writing a book about a personality disorder, as I've said, is that it can be a means of exercising power over another, the exact opposite impetus of Paul's visionary words. To be sure, a diagnosis can be a means of clarity, even hope, and possibly healing. But if we have not navigated our own woundedness, it can be a means of judgment and a cheap form of self-satisfaction. I know because I lived like this for years after a terribly painful event that I refused to properly grieve and heal from, in exchange for the faux power of vindictive rage, judgment, and a label for the one who hurt me.

I long to live as a participant in a new order of things, a radical way of lamentation and repentance, forgiveness and surrender, hope and healing. In reality, though, I continue to live between the old order of rage and judgment and this new, redemptive order. We all do. My clients who have suffered under the spiritual, emotional, or sexual abuse of a narcissist remind me that the journey from the chains of slavery to the freedom of faith, hope, and love is a long and challenging one. But I must always hold out the promise of a life beyond the old order, an order that seems to feed our appetite for polarization and victimization and authoritarianism and everything else that robs freedom and joy.

A gracious friend who read my work recently said to me, "Chuck, this is really the story of all of us." My hope is that you've seen yourself in these pages, and that it's prompted self-reflection, honest repentance, and relational reconciliation. I'm quite sure you've also seen many others in these pages too. And I pray that I've offered a profoundly honest, serious, and challenging assessment for you, for them, and for the church. My greatest hope is that this reading leads you into humility, the "mindset of Jesus Christ," which allows for both an honest assessment of the violence we experience and a redemptive pathway through it.

The way of Jesus is the only way I know that holds the tension, that offers us the gift of feeling our anger without being enslaved to it, that offers the honesty of naming violence without resorting to it, that offers the promise of hope without cheapening it. I long for that way, even if the journey to it is long and winding.

ACKNOWLEDGMENTS

Years ago, a friend challenged me—"You're always quoting others. . . . Trust your own voice." While I think I've discovered something of my own voice, I can't help but acknowledge the "cloud of witnesses" without whose wisdom this book would be hopelessly deficient.

I've been reading and learning from Diane Langberg and Dan Allender since the mid-1990s—where do their voices end and mine begin? If you listen carefully, you'll hear echoes of a diverse array of theological and pastoral voices—Spurgeon and Merton, Buechner and Peterson, Nouwen and B. B. Taylor. You won't see it, but you'll rightly assume that poets and novelists and trauma theorists are stacked on my nightstand. You'll wonder how someone can read Carl Jung and Richard Rohr and Mary Oliver alongside St. Augustine and John Calvin.

You don't know them, but you'd do well to whisper a thank you to the many souls I've worked with as a pastor, therapist, spiritual director, consultant, and retreat leader. I think of a woman who shared her story after an evening session during a west coast trip. It was late and I was exhausted and yet honored and compelled by her story of courage in the face of narcissistic abuse. That night, she became my teacher, reminding me to write from a place of hope, not cynicism. Even more recently, clients have said, "This is what has helped" and "Make sure you say this." I'm so thankful for everyone I've had the privilege of pastoring and counseling over the years.

I'm grateful beyond words for my wife, Sara, and my daughters, Emma and Maggie, for supporting my sometimes hard-to-describe vocation. I get to teach and write and travel, all with deep support from my girls, whose love for me and even honesty with me reminds me that my own work is never done. Life with them is just good, profoundly and astonishingly good.

I give thanks to God for Western Theological Seminary and its support for my vocation. I have extraordinary staff and faculty colleagues, as well as students who challenge me and chide me and teach me too. They've shown such great interest in this topic. I've been energized by all of them.

A providential encounter with IVP's publisher, Jeff Crosby, led to a book proposal and a new publishing relationship for me, and it's been deeply satisfying. Ethan McCarthy's fine editing and wise insights further honed the work, and the whole team's support is gratifying.

Finally, as I round the corner of fifty years old, I find myself sitting with Jesus more closely than I did even a decade ago. The compassionate, humble Savior of the world didn't scheme, showed no grandiosity, and loved courageously, revealing the heart of God. I'm more convinced today that his smile is the deep cure for our pervasive shame. I rest in the love of one who sees me, even when I hide, pursuing boundlessly. I have unrelenting hope because nothing can ultimately separate us from his infinitely available love.

APPENDIX

Engaging the Nine Faces of Narcissism—
Strategies for Therapists, Pastors,
and Friends Who Care

TYPE TWO: THE SAVIOR

When engaging and interacting with a benevolent narcissist, we need to remember that buried in her heart is a cauldron of unmet needs. She longs to be loved, but sabotages love through her relentless, ingratiating behavior. Her quiet cry is "Love me, love me!" even if she's giving, helping, and offering herself. She may be so defended that any hint you give that she has been hurtful or harmful in her intention or impact may sabotage dialogue.

When I work with someone like this, I'll often say something like, "Let's make a deal. For this hour, you don't have to take care of anyone, including me." When she inevitably turns it back on me, I'll remind her of our deal. As we get more honest, I describe the impact of her unsolicited attempts to caretake. Ultimately, I want her to know that she sabotages the real connection she longs for.

Remember, in losing her capacity to help, she feels like she is losing the most vital part of herself. Though pride is the root sin of this face of narcissism, shame lurks underneath, and to avoid it she turns outward, to the other. This is her *modus operandi,* and for those cut off from their deep, true selves anchored in God's love, this may be the only self they know. You may find compassion for her when you remember how threatening it may feel to her to relax that benevolently narcissistic part of herself. She's never really been known for anything else.

TYPE THREE: THE WINNER

Confident and self-assured, this face of narcissism is well defended against anything that threatens his shiny veneer. But life lived on stage can be lonely and exhausting, and the hope of breaking through to his heart may lie in his desire for a respite from the gauntlet of achievement.

When I work with individuals like this, it helps me to remember that they are far more anxious than I think. Though they appear poised, they are fearful of failure. Though put together, they're quite exhausted. And so I propose an agreement of sorts, saying, "For one hour each week, invite me backstage, behind the curtain, out of the spotlight, so that I can see and hear the real you."

Each of us longs to be known for who we are. And even though this face of narcissism may be the brightest and shiniest of them all, he too longs to be known for more than his outward façade. The root sin of deceit is really a coping strategy, a way of defending himself against being seen as wounded, fragile, a failure. He deceives by splitting off his shadow self, but his own strategy for self-protection becomes a strategy he employs in all relationships.

You offer him the prospect of hope by giving him one relationship where he can relax his strategies and risk being fully known. He'll dodge and evade, and he'll likely play his habitual game with you, but if you can endure, you may be allowed backstage, into the beauty of his brokenness.

TYPE FOUR: THE INDIVIDUALIST

Loving this person can be tricky, because her capacity for emotion may actually be an obstacle to connection. And while she feels like she is the most emotionally available person the world has ever known, her emotionality and dramatic style may actually be a strategy for keeping you close but not too close.

I often imagine the metaphor of a hurricane when I think of this relational strategy. The unique aircrafts called "Hurricane Hunters" often capture images of the beauty and complexity of the hurricane, but few pilots enjoy entering into the chaotic winds of the storm. The question is, are you willing to enter in? And will you not mistake the dramatic winds for the quiet eye of the storm?

This person trades ordinary, healthy love for the intense and dramatic, so the deal I make is this: "Will you allow me to believe, and even to see, that you are more than your dramatic swirling winds? Will you allow to me into the quiet, tender, vulnerable eye of the storm?" I know she longs to be seen and understood, but I want her to know that she doesn't have to work so hard for it. She's worth knowing, seeing, pursuing, and loving. But she likely doesn't believe there is anything but the hurricane.

I've found that those who live from this narcissistic face are often exhausted, and they're not sure why. If they realize that there is freedom from the drama that occupies so much inner space and relational energy, they'll find vigor and resilience they didn't know was possible.

TYPE FIVE: THE DISTANCER

As the intellectualizing narcissist, this person goes to great lengths to protect himself from anything or anyone that threatens his omniscience. His coping strategy of intellectualizing has kept him safe in a world that is scary and unpredictable, so relaxing this part of him feels quite risky.

When I'm working with folks like this, I need to be patient. Feelings can't be forced or compelled. Indeed, just the fact that he's sitting with another human being might be progress, as he's safest in the control tower of his own head.

The deal I make with him goes something like this: "When we discover you don't know it all, I promise that I won't leave, mock you, or think less of you." I like to value their intelligence, not as a strategy, but out of genuine appreciation for just how smart and thoughtful they can be. And yet, perhaps the deepest shame is what they don't know—they don't how to relate, how to connect. And so, if you can build trust, you can engage their God-gifted intelligence wisely. You may offer a book resource. I often recommend Curt Thompson's *Anatomy of the Soul* or Dan Allender's *The Cry of the Soul: How Our Emotions Reveal Our Deepest Questions About God,* proposing to them that it might be easier to talk about and study emotions before delving in.

When I do get a small glimpse into emotion, I'm not quick to pounce or call attention, but I might just wait until the end of our time to say, "I noticed that you teared up a bit today talking about your Dad. Thank you." I want to convey commitment to the relationship more than some display of emotion. Transformation will be slow, with tentative awakenings to his strategies for survival. I remind myself that I'm committed not to instant transformation, but to slow and incremental change.

TYPE SIX: THE HAWKEYE

The anxious, hypervigilant narcissist can be wearying to relate to at times, as it feels like she is constantly watching, perpetually evaluating. New therapists often feel inadequate with clients like this. Pastors may feel evaluated. Friends may grow tired of constant criticism of them or others.

If you respond in kind with a critique of her habits, you'll be rebuked quickly. In this, you'd do well to recognize that she's actually quite anxious, and even more, quite exhausted in her anxiety. Her controlling, vigilant habits are attempts to keep the anxiety at bay. Arguing, confronting, or criticizing only serves to heighten her anxiety.

I often say, "I want our space together to be a space of peace for you, a space where you can relax and feel safe." That is a wondrous invitation for someone whose life feels anything but peaceful. However, those who are narcissistic will resist this invitation to relax, to surrender, and instead sabotage your invitation. They may feign cooperation in your invitation to growth out of loyalty to you or to a process, showing up to meet you regularly but not surrendering their anxiety at a deeper level. It may take a significant amount of time for them to relax, fully allowing themselves to trust you. In this space of trust, they may finally let their guard down enough to receive honest feedback about how their way of relating hurts them and others.

TYPE SEVEN: THE OPTIMIST

Like a frog dancing across lily pads, this hedonistic narcissistic will jump from one experience or pleasure to another to avoid the real pain of his life. He'll seem as if he is fine. He'll turn your frown upside down, as they say. But you'll walk away wondering what's really going on below the surface.

My invitation for this person is to stop long enough to be known. I might say, "I'd love for our time together to be one space in your life where you can step off of the hamster wheel, take a deep breath, and feel." Their perpetual motion keeps them from feeling their pain, their sadness, their loneliness, their ache for something more than immediate gratification. And so, we must appreciate the great risk it is for them to stop and be still, even for just a few moments.

This face of narcissism is appealing, charming, and engaging, so much so that those in his narcissistic path may question their own perception or judgment of the person or situation. We care for them by refusing to believe this is all there is. We create a space where their habitual patterns can be relaxed and where they can be truly known. In time they may express their weariness of life lived on the hamster wheel and take stock of its cost to them and others.

It helps me to remember that there is sadness beneath their optimistic veneer. I feel compassion for them when I realize that their frenetic, even addictive, pace and habits mask a deep ache. My commitment is to hold this truth, even when they don't.

TYPE EIGHT: THE CHALLENGER

Most in the path of the narcissistic challenger feel blown down like trees by a tornado. He can be forceful, relentless, profoundly unaware of the extent of his strength. He may be dismissed as a bully, as arrogant, as shameless.

And yet he longs for someone to enter into his powerful energy field, to risk connection. Like Lennie in *Of Mice and Men,* he longs to hug and hold and squeeze, but may be unaware of his own power. Most don't realize that the majority of people in the world don't feel the immense energy in their being that they feel.

My compassion grows as I realize that the challenger is really a little boy or girl longing for love, to be seen and known. My role is to step courageously into relationship, not as a wallflower (or he won't respect me) but as one willing to wrestle, even to confront. In the relationship, I display a safe strength, modeling vulnerability while at the same time creating what therapists call a "holding environment" for his strength and energy. When the challenger experiences this, he is more apt to relax a bit, to open up, to acknowledge his impact on others.

Deep down, this is a person who does not want you to reduce them to one common denominator, emotion, or characteristic—namely, anger. My deal for them: "Let's agree that you are angry, but anger isn't all you are, and let's listen to the story of your anger together."

TYPE NINE: THE WALLFLOWER

The passive-aggressive narcissist is the most subtle of all, as we saw earlier in the book. In unhealth, she seethes with quiet rage. Her narcissism is far from grandiose, but she wields a power that leaves others walking on eggshells and wondering how to help or care. At her most unaware, she is a walking paradox—the Enneagram type that at her best is a healing peacemaker is, in this unhealthy place, brooding and demanding and perpetually angst filled. In this place, they may convey: "I want you near, but I don't want you close."

One must be patient and committed when loving this person, because you are journeying into territory that is utterly unfamiliar to them. Disconnected from a rich inner life, they live as lonely orphans, wandering the earth looking for a faithful companion. You can offer a meaningful companionship, but it will require a fierce intentionality, a desire to press past their defenses into their lost inner world.

They may be surprisingly defensive when asked to consider how they hurt others. Keep in mind that they lack insight into themselves and their relational patterns. They are better able to name outer dynamics than inner dynamics. They see life through the lens of others. So my offer to them is this: "If you risk letting me pursue you, I promise to be gentle, to ask permission, but to press in further even when you resist." Someone who wants to grow will receive this offer.

TYPE ONE: THE PERFECTIONIST

The perfectionistic narcissist is always right, so blinded by certitude that curiosity about his inner life and impact is difficult. This face of narcissism protects him from the messy and gray contingencies of life, from the chaos that lies underneath. My compassion grows when I realize that he needs to split life into binaries in order to exist—black and white, good and bad, right and wrong. It protects him from the chaotic feelings within.

This kind of narcissist may feel utterly certain about the injustices and wrongs in the world around them but experience anxiety and shame about their own inner wrongness. They order their external world to pacify an inner disorder. Demanding rightness out there allows me to ignore wrongness within me. Demanding goodness out there allows me to ignore badness within me.

One way I help him is to create a space where he can experience a respite from himself and from the broken world in which he lives. I create a peaceful space for him. I choose not to enter into a debate, even if he tries. I refuse to play his game. I may even say, "I'm not here to debate you. Maybe this can be one relationship where you can relax." The more narcissistic he is, the more unwilling he'll be to relax, even to cooperate. He may even find things wrong in what you say or how you facilitate the time. Don't be baited into a debate, though. That only perpetuates the cycle and fuels his self-evasion.

I want to acknowledge his longing for a just and ordered world. His stifling anxiety and simmering frustration mask a deeper longing for the true, the good, and the beautiful. This is a good longing. However, he sabotages it as he tries to control the outcome. Like an addict, he must get to the point of acknowledging his powerlessness, relinquishing control so that he can experience the joy of longing without the certainty of an outcome.

NOTES

INTRODUCTION

[1]Brittany Cassell, "Johns Hopkins' Top Psychotherapist Releases Terrifying Diagnosis of President Trump," *Bipartisan Report*, January 27, 2017, http://bipartisanreport.com/2017/01/27/johns-hopkins-top-psychotherapist-releases-terrifying-diagnosis-of-president-trump/.

[2]Christopher Lasch, *The Culture of Narcissism: American Life in an Age of Diminishing Expectations* (New York: Norton, 1979), 241.

[3]If I share stories of my personal experience with narcissistic leadership in this book, I keep them sufficiently vague as to not relitigate past confrontations, old wounds, and (in some cases) helpful reconciliations. Ultimately, this book is not about my story, but *our* shared story of narcissism.

[4]Donald Capps, *The Depleted Self: Sin in a Narcissistic Age* (Minneapolis: Augsburg, 1993).

[5]See Terrence Real, *I Don't Want to Talk About It: Overcoming the Secret Legacy of Male Depression* (New York: Scribner, 1998), for a compelling account of the misdiagnosis of male depression and its relationship to shame, addiction, and narcissism.

[6]Alexander Lowen, *Narcissism: Denial of the True Self* (New York: Touchstone, 1985).

[7]Eugene Peterson, *Earth and Altar: The Community of Prayer in a Self-Bound Society* (Downers Grove, IL: InterVarsity Press, 1985).

[8]Jean M. Twenge and W. Keith Campbell, *The Narcissism Epidemic: Living in the Age of Entitlement* (New York: Simon & Schuster, 2009).

[9]F. S. Stinson et al., "Prevalence, Correlates, Disability, and Comorbidity of DSM-IV Narcissistic Personality Disorder," *Journal of Clinical Psychiatry* 7 (2008): 1033-45, www.ncbi.nlm.nih.gov/pubmed/18557663.

[10]Jeremy Dean, "The Dangerous Personality Trait on the Rise in the Young," *PsyBlog* (blog), September 20, 2016, www.spring.org.uk/2016/09/personality -trait-leads-chronic-disappointment.php; Joel Stein, "Millennials: The Me Me Me Generation," *Time*, May 20, 2013, http://time.com/247/millennials-the -me-me-me-generation/.

[11]Larry Alton, "Millennials and Entitlement in the Workplace: The Good, the Bad, and the Ugly," *Forbes*, November 22, 2017, www.forbes.com/sites/larry alton/2017/11/22/millennials-and-entitlement-in-the-workplace-the-good -the-bad-and-the-ugly/.

[12]For a critique of the theory behind *The Narcissism Epidemic*, see Craig Malkin, *Rethinking Narcissism: The Bad—and Surprising Good—About Feeling Special* (New York: Harper, 2015).

[13]"Daily Affirmation with Stuart Smalley," comedy sketch, *Saturday Night Live*, season 16, episode 12, aired February 9, 1991, on NBC.

[14]See James Masterson, *Search for the Real Self: Unmasking the Personality Disorders of Our Age* (New York: Free Press, 1988).

[15]Thomas Merton, *New Seeds of Contemplation* (New York: New Directions, 2007), 34.

[16]Frederick Buechner, *Telling Secrets: A Memoir* (New York: Harper Collins, 1991), 45.

[17]Elinor Greenberg, *Borderline, Narcissistic, and Schizoid Adaptations: The Pursuit of Love, Admiration, and Safety* (Createspace Independent Publishing Platform, 2016), 3. Thanks to my friend, the writer and therapist Heather Drew, for introducing me to this helpful book.

1 WHEN NARCISSISM COMES TO CHURCH

[1]Diane Langberg, "Narcissism and the Systems It Breeds," lecture for the Forum of Christian Leaders, video, 1:05:52, published May 5, 2016, www.youtube .com/watch?v=4BU3pwBa0qU.

[2]Charles Haddon Spurgeon, "A Divided Heart," sermon, September 25, 1859, Spurgeon Center Resource Library, www.spurgeon.org/resource-library /sermons/a-divided-heart.

[3]To protect the stories and identities of people I've worked with over the years, I do not merely change names but craft new stories that contain characteristics of several different encounters. Any recognition of one's story in this book is mere coincidence.

[4]Henri Nouwen, *In The Name of Jesus: Reflections on Christian Leadership* (Chestnut Ridge, NY: Crossroad, 1989), 60.

[5]Susan Howatch, *Glittering Images* (New York: Ballantine, 1987).

⁶Sarah Eekhoff Zylstra, "The 8 People Americans Trust More Than Their Local Pastor," *Christianity Today*, January 8, 2018, www.christianitytoday.com/news/2018 /january/8-people-americans-trust-more-than-their-local-pastor.html.

⁷See Yonat Shimron, "More Seminary Students Leave the Master of Divinity Behind," *Religion News Service*, May 11, 2018, https://religionnews.com/2018 /05/11/more-seminary-students-leave-the-master-of-divinity-behind/.

⁸See Harry Bruinius, "Amid Evangelical Decline, Growing Split Between Young Christians and Church Leaders," *Christian Science Monitor*, October 10, 2017, www.csmonitor.com/USA/Politics/2017/1010/Amid-Evangelical-decline -growing-split-between-young-Christians-and-church-elders/.

⁹For more on these historical developments and this "kenotic configuration," see Roger Haydon Mitchell, *Church, Gospel, and Empire: How the Politics of Sovereignty Impregnated the West* (Eugene, OR: Wipf and Stock, 2011).

¹⁰See Tim Stevens, "Mark Driscoll and Other Narcissistic Pastors," *LeadingSmart*, September 2, 2014, http://leadingsmart.com/leadingsmart/2014/8/mark -driscoll-and-other-narcissistic-pastors.

¹¹For more on patriarchal systems and how they perpetuate abuse against women, see Janet Jacobs, "Charisma, Male Entitlement, and the Abuse of Power," in *Bad Pastors: Clergy Misconduct in Modern America*, ed. Anson D. Shupe, William A. Stacey, and Susan E. Darnell (New York: NYU Press, 2000).

¹²Jerrold Post, "Narcissism and the Charismatic Leader-Follower Relationship," *Political Psychology* 7, no. 4 (1986): 675.

¹³Walter Brueggemann, *The Prophetic Imagination*, 2nd ed. (Minneapolis: Fortress, 2001), 92.

2 UNDERSTANDING NARCISSISM

¹Material in this section first appeared on the author's website. Chuck DeGroat, "The Myth of Narcissus and the Hope of Redemption," *Becoming Yourself* (blog), July 25, 2018, https://chuckdegroat.net/2018/07/25/the-myth-of-narcissus -and-the-hope-of-redemption/.

²Terrence Real, *I Don't Want to Talk About It: Overcoming the Secret Legacy of Male Depression* (New York: Scribner, 1998), loc. 526-30, Kindle.

³John Bradshaw, *Healing the Shame That Binds You* (Deerfield Beach, FL: Health Communications, 2005), 34.

⁴Being turned in on oneself is actually an ancient understanding of human sin, as seen in Augustine's use of the Latin phrase *homo incurvatus in se,* a concept that was then formalized by Martin Luther during the Protestant Reformation.

⁵For more on how our bodies process trauma, see the groundbreaking work of Peter Levine, especially his *Waking the Tiger: Healing Trauma* (Berkeley, CA:

North Atlantic, 1997). Unprocessed trauma often needs a release event, but these moments can be triggered by destabilizing life events.

[6]For a more extensive introduction to this debate, see Craig Malkin, *Rethinking Narcissism: The Bad—and Surprising Good—About Feeling Special* (New York: Harper, 2015), 16-23.

[7]American Psychiatric Association, "DSM-IV and DSM-5 Criteria for the Personality Disorders" (2012), www.psi.uba.ar/academica/carrerasdegrado /psicologiasitios_catedras/practicas_profesionales/820_clinica_tr_person alidad_psicosis/material/dsm.pdf.

[8]P. J. Watson, "Complexity of Narcissism and a Continuum of Self-Esteem Regulation," in *Personality Disorders,* Evidence and Experience in Psychiatry 8, ed. Mario Maj (New York: Wiley, 2005), 336-38. For a more popular rendition, see Malkin, *Rethinking Narcissism,* chap. 3.

[9]For a secular appraisal of healthy narcissism, see Susan Kolod, "What Is Healthy Narcissism?" *Psychology Today* (blog), September 26, 2016, www .psychologytoday.com/us/blog/contemporary-psychoanalysis-in-action/201609 /what-is-healthy-narcissism.

[10]I use these categories frequently in my clinical assessments of pastoral candidates when I administer the Millon Clinical Multiaxial Inventory (MCMI-IV), which is based on the research of Theodore Millon, PhD.

[11]Most notably, see James Masterson, *Search for the Real Self: Unmasking the Personality Disorders of Our Age* (New York: Free Press, 1988).

[12]Aaron L. Pincus and Michael J. Roche, "Narcissistic Grandiosity and Narcissistic Vulnerability," in *The Handbook of Narcissism and Narcissistic Personality Disorder: Theoretical Approaches, Empirical Findings, and Treatments,* ed. W. Keith Campbell and Joshua D. Miller (Hoboken, NJ: Wiley and Sons, 2011).

[13]M. J. Horowitz, "Clinical Phenomenology of Narcissistic Pathology," *Psychiatric Clinics of North America* 12, no. 3 (September 1989): 531-39.

[14]See, e.g., Preston Ni, "7 Signs of a Covert Introvert Narcissist," *Psychology Today* (blog), January 10, 2016, www.psychologytoday.com/us/blog/communication -success/201601/7-signs-covert-introvert-narcissist.

[15]See Aaron L. Pincus and Mark R. Lukowitsky, "Pathological Narcissism and Narcissistic Personality Disorder," *Annual Review of Clinical Psychology* 6: 8.1- 8.21 (2010), https://pdfs.semanticscholar.org/b407/2db2b0bf23f61f8913d3 05ce22fef4bda677.pdf.

[16]David M. Buss and Lisa Chiodo also provide helpful categories that show a range of narcissistic dispositions and the consequent actions that may result.

These seven dispositions manifest as the primary relational styles we lead with in our everyday life. "Narcissistic Acts in Everyday Life," *Journal of Personality* 59, no. 2 (June 1991): 179-215.

[17]If you'd like to step away from popular online articles into solid theory, your first purchase should be Campbell and Miller, *Handbook of Narcissism.*

[18]For more on this, see my book *Toughest People to Love: How to Understand, Lead, and Love the Difficult People in Your Life—Including Yourself* (Grand Rapids: Eerdmans, 2014).

[19]See Otto Kernberg, *Aggressivity, Narcissism, and Self-Destructiveness in the Psychotherapeutic Relationship: New Developments in the Psychopathology and Psychotherapy of Severe Personality Disorders* (New Haven, CT: Yale University Press, 2004).

[20]Gregory of Nyssa, *Homilies on the Beatitudes: An English Version with Commentary and Supporting Studies*, ed. Hubertus R. Drobner and Alberto Viciano (Leiden: Brill, 2000), 70.

[21]For a compelling profile of the cycle of addiction, see Patrick Carnes, *Out of the Shadows: Facing Sexual Addiction* (Center City, MN: Hazeldon, 1983).

[22]Thomas J. Scheff, "Shame and the Social Bond: A Sociological Theory," accessed August 11, 2019, www.soc.ucsb.edu/faculty/scheff/main.php?id=2.html.

[23]See Patricia DeYoung, *Understanding and Treating Chronic Shame: A Relational/Neurobiological Approach* (New York: Routledge, 2015).

[24]Pia Mellody's work on abuse and addiction is helpful. She often talks about a kind of disempowering abuse that leads to shame and victimization, and a false empowering abuse that leads to shamelessness and grandiosity. Both are problematic for a child who grows up looking for the authentic love she needed in addictions.

3 THE NINE FACES OF NARCISSISM

[1]Thomas Merton, *Raids on the Unspeakable* (New York: New Directions, 1966), 15-16.

[2]For a helpful discussion of this dynamic, see Christopher L. Heuertz, *The Sacred Enneagram: Finding Your Unique Path to Spiritual Growth* (Grand Rapids: Zondervan, 2017).

[3]Wendy Farley, *The Wounding and Healing of Desire: Weaving Heaven and Earth* (Louisville, KY: Westminster John Knox, 2005), 47.

[4]For a brief summary, see Richard Rohr, "Belly, Heart, and Head," Center for Action and Contemplation, April 26, 2016, https://cac.org/belly-heart-head-2016-04-26/.

[5]See Elsa Ronningstam, "Psychoanalytic Theories on Narcissism and Narcissistic Personality," in *The Handbook of Narcissism and Narcissistic Personality Disorder: Theoretical Approaches, Empirical Findings, and Treatments,* ed. W. Keith Campbell and Joshua D. Miller (Hoboken, NJ: Wiley and Sons, 2011).

[6]See Thomas Keating, *The Human Condition: Contemplation and Transformation* (Mahwah, NJ: Paulist, 1999).

[7]For those who've interacted with the Enneagram in depth, I welcome critique and clarification.

[8]Marva Dawn and Eugene Peterson, *The Unnecessary Pastor: Rediscovering the Call* (Grand Rapids: Eerdmans, 1999), 14.

[9]See C. A. Darling, E. W. Hill, and L. M. McWey, "Understanding Stress and Quality of Life for Clergy and Clergy Spouses," *Stress and Health* 20, no. 5 (October 2004): 261-77; and S. S. Ferguson, "Clergy Compassion Fatigue," *Family Therapy Magazine* 2 (2007): 16-18.

[10]My thanks to Michael Cusick for this language he offered in a brief conversation about narcissism and Enneagram Type Twos.

[11]Heinz Kohut, "Narcissism and Narcissistic Rage," *Psychoanalytic Study of the Child* 27 (1972): 379-92.

[12]F. LeRon Schults and Steven J. Sandage, *The Faces of Forgiveness: Searching for Wholeness and Salvation* (Grand Rapids: Baker, 2003), 57.

[13]Thomas Merton, *No Man Is an Island* (New York: Shambhala, 1955), 119.

[14]Alice Miller, *The Drama of the Gifted Child: The Search for the True Self* (New York: Basic Books, 1997), 112.

[15]Evagrius Ponticus, *The Praktikos,* 120.

[16]Glen O. Gabbard, "Two Subtypes of Narcissistic Personality Disorder," *Bulletin of the Menninger Clinic* 53, no. 6 (November 1989): 527-32.

[17]Don Richard Riso and Russ Hudson, "The Loyalist: Enneagram Type Six," Enneagram Institute, accessed August 11, 2019, www.enneagraminstitute.com/type-6.

[18]Claudio Naranjo, *Character and Neurosis: An Integrative View* (Nevada City, CA: Gateways/IDHHB, 1994).

[19]Henri Nouwen, *Out of Solitude: Three Meditations of the Christian Life* (Notre Dame, IN: Ave Maria, 2004), 28.

[20]Abba Poemen, cited in Yushi Nomura, *Desert Wisdom: The Sayings of the Desert Fathers* (Maryknoll, NY: Orbis, 2001), 83.

[21]Susan Krauss Whitbourne, "Why It's So Hard to Live with Narcissists," *Psychology Today* (blog), July 12, 2014, www.psychologytoday.com/blog/fulfillment-any-age/201407/why-its-so-hard-live-with-narcissists.

[22]Steven Sandage and Shane Moe, "Narcissism and Spirituality," in Campbell and Miller, *Handbook of Narcissism*, 414.

4 CHARACTERISTICS OF THE NARCISSISTIC PASTOR

[1]Diane Langberg, "Narcissism and the Systems It Breeds," lecture for the Forum of Christian Leaders, video, 1:05:52, published May 5, 2016, www.youtube.com/watch?v=4BU3pwBa0qU.

[2]William N. Grosch, "Narcissism: Shame, Rage and Addiction," *Psychiatric Quarterly* 65, no. 1 (1994): 49.

[3]For statistics, see Pastoral Care Inc. Staff, "Pastoral Addictions: Do Pastors Struggle with Addictions," accessed August 11, 2019, www.pastoralcareinc.com/pastoral-addictions/.

[4]Christopher Lasch, *The Culture of Narcissism: American Life in an Age of Diminishing Expectations* (New York: Norton, 1979), 86.

[5]Craig and Carolyn Williford, *How to Treat a Staff Infection: Resolving Problems in Your Church or Ministry* (Grand Rapids: Baker, 2006), 104-10.

[6]Recounted in Eugene Peterson, *Under the Unpredictable Plant: An Exploration in Vocational Holiness* (Grand Rapids: Eerdmans, 1992).

[7]Langberg, "Narcissism and the Systems It Breeds."

[8]See Aaron L. Pincus and Michael J. Roche, "Narcissistic Grandiosity and Narcissistic Vulnerability," in *The Handbook of Narcissism and Narcissistic Personality Disorder: Theoretical Approaches, Empirical Findings, and Treatments*, ed. W. Keith Campbell and Joshua D. Miller (Hoboken, NJ: Wiley and Sons, 2011).

[9]Material in this section is adapted from Chuck DeGroat, "Fauxnerability in the Church: What Is It? What Do We Do About It?," *Becoming Yourself* (blog), June 11, 2018, https://chuckdegroat.net/2018/06/11/fauxnerability-in-the-church-what-is-it-what-do-we-do-about-it/.

5 THE INNER LIFE OF A NARCISSISTIC PASTOR

[1]Rainer Maria Rilke, *Letters to a Young Poet,* trans. Charlie Louth (New York: Penguin, 2013), 56.

[2]Terrence Real, *I Don't Want to Talk About It: Overcoming the Secret Legacy of Male Depression* (New York: Scribner, 1998), loc. 225-26, Kindle.

[3]See Carl Jung, *Modern Man in Search of a Soul* (New York: Martino, 2017).

[4]See "The Johari Window," Changing Minds, accessed August 11, 2019, http://changingminds.org/disciplines/communication/models/johari_window.htm.

[5]Some of the best resources for doing this shadow work come from a newer modality called "internal family systems theory," a perspective I share in my

book *Wholeheartedness: Busyness, Exhaustion, and Healing the Divided Self* (Grand Rapids: Eerdmans, 2016).

[6]I'm mindful of New Life Church in New York City (newlife.nyc) where for many years under the leadership of Pete Scazzero, and now Rich Villodas, this work has been fundamental to their ministry and mission both personally and organizationally.

6 UNDERSTANDING NARCISSISTIC SYSTEMS

[1]Ronald Heifetz, *The Practice of Adaptive Leadership* (Boston: Cambridge Leadership Associates, 2009), 7.

[2]Triangulation occurs when someone refuses to deal directly with the person they're struggling with and instead enjoins a third person to alleviate the anxiety for them.

[3]A. G. de Zavala, "Collective Narcissism and Its Social Consequences," *Journal of Personality and Social Psychology* 97, no. 6 (2009): 1074-96.

[4]See Dennis Duchon and Michael Burns, "Organizational Narcissism," *Organizational Dynamics* 37, no. 4 (October–December 2008): 354-64.

[5]See Jim Herrington, Mike Bonem, and James Furr, *Leading Congregational Change: A Practical Guide for the Transformational Journey* (New York: Jossey-Bass, 2000).

[6]Duchon and Burns, "Organizational Narcissism," 355.

[7]Duchon and Burns, "Organizational Narcissism," 361.

[8]See Ed Stetzer's three-part series, "Considering (and Surviving) Unhealthy Christian Organizations," *The Exchange* (blog), April 5, 2012 (part 1), April 10, 2012 (part 2), June 26, 2012 (part 3), www.christianitytoday.com /edstetzer/2012/april/considering-and-surviving-unhealthy-christian.html.

[9]See "About," on Sharon Hersh's official website, accessed August 11, 2019, www .sharonhersh.com/about/.

7 THE GASLIGHT IS ON: SPIRITUAL AND EMOTIONAL ABUSE

[1]See Patricia Evans's helpful book *Controlling People: How to Recognize, Understand, and Deal with People Who Try to Control You* (Avon, MA: Adams, 2002), where she describes the "Teddy Syndrome."

[2]For a helpful, descriptive list, see "Emotional Abuse," Out of the FOG, accessed August 11, 2019, http://outofthefog.website/top-100-trait-blog/2015/11/4 /emotional-abuse.

[3]Daniel Shaw, *Traumatizing Narcissism: Relational Systems of Subjugation* (New York: Routledge, 2014), 71.

[4]Peter Levine, *Healing Trauma: A Pioneering Program for Restoring the Wisdom of Your Body* (Boulder, CO: Sounds True, 2008), 30.

[5]Bessel van der Kolk, *The Body Keeps the Score: Brain, Mind, and Body in the Healing of Trauma* (New York: Penguin, 2014), 90.

[6]Peter Levine, *In an Unspoken Voice: How the Body Releases Trauma and Restores Goodness* (Berkeley, CA: North Atlantic, 2010), xii.

[7]To understand the dynamics of narcissistic family systems and their impact in the present, see Stephanie Donald-Pressman and Robert Pressman, *The Narcissistic Family: Diagnosis and Treatment* (New York: Jossey-Bass, 1994).

[8]Van der Kolk, *Body Keeps the Score*, 97.

8 HEALING OURSELVES, HEALING THE CHURCH

[1]For a helpful look at empathy and narcissism, see Hessel Zondag, "Unconditional Giving and Unconditional Taking: Empathy and Narcissism Among Pastors," *Journal of Pastoral Care and Counseling* 61, nos. 1-2 (Spring-Summer 2007): 85-97.

[2]Lesslie Newbigin, *The Good Shepherd: Meditations on Christian Ministry in Today's World* (Grand Rapids: Eerdmans, 1977), 56-57.

[3]Robert Quinn, *Deep Change: Discovering the Leader Within* (San Francisco: Jossey-Bass, 1996).

[4]See Peter Levine, *Healing Trauma: A Pioneering Program for Restoring the Wisdom of Your Body* (Boulder, CO: Sounds True, 2008).

[5]See Mark Banschick, "Somatic Experiencing: How Trauma Can Be Overcome," *Psychology Today* (blog), March 26, 2015, www.psychologytoday.com/us/blog /the-intelligent-divorce/201503/somatic-experiencing.

[6]For a helpful biblical understanding of divorce and the church, see David Instone-Brewer, *Divorce and Remarriage in the Church: Biblical Solutions for Pastoral Realities* (Downers Grove, IL: InterVarsity Press, 2003).

9 TRANSFORMATION FOR NARCISSISTS (IS POSSIBLE)

[1]John O'Donohue, *The Inner Landscape,* audio recording (Boulder, CO: Sounds True, 1997).

[2]Macarius, *Homily XV, The Art of Prayer: An Orthodox Anthology*, ed. Igumen Chariton of Valemo (London: Faber and Faber, 1966), 18.

[3]See the official website of the Center for Self Leadership at www.selfleadership .org for more information.

[4]Susan Howatch, *Glittering Images* (New York: Ballantine, 1987), 224.

[5]P. J. Watson and Michael D. Biderman, "Narcissistic Personality Inventory Factors, Splitting, and Self-Consciousness," *Journal of Personality Assessment* 61 (1993): 41-57.

[6]Sr. Jean Marie Dwyer, *The Unfolding Journey: The God Within: Etty Hillesum and Meister Eckhart* (Toronto: Novalis, 2014), loc. 868-69, Kindle.

[7]Etty Hillesum, *The Letters and Diaries of Etty Hillesum* (Grand Rapids: Eerdmans, 2002), 465.

[8]Patrick Woodhouse, *Etty Hillesum: A Life Transformed* (New York: Continuum, 2009), 145.

EPILOGUE: HE HUMBLED HIMSELF . . .

[1]See Thomas Keating, *On Divine Therapy* (New York: Lantern, 2012).

[2]It's also striking to me that Paul's conversion process, while seemingly instantaneous, requires three years in a wilderness, a place of refinement. Real change takes significant time.